1599   Moved to Southwark near the Globe Theatre which he and his company had recently erected.

1602   Extensive purchases of property and land in Stratford.

1602–4 Lodged v   ee and a maker of   ndon. Helped to arrange   Mary Mountjoy   pprentice.

1603   His company became the King's Majesty's Players under royal patronage.

1607   His daughter Susanna married Dr John Hall.

1608   Birth of Shakespeare's grand-daughter Elizabeth Hall.

1610   Shakespeare possibly returned to live in Stratford.

1613   Purchase of the Gatehouse in Blackfriars. Burning of the Globe Theatre during the première of *Henry VIII*.

1616   Marriage of his daughter Judith to Thomas Quiney in Lent for which they were excommunicated.

25 March, 1616   Shakespeare altered the draft of his will presumably to give Judith more security in view of her husband's unreliability and his pre-marital misconduct with another woman. His will also revealed his strong attachment to his Stratford friends, and above all his desire to arrange for the establishment of his descendants.

23 April, 1616   Death of Shakespeare.

1623   Publication of the First Folio edition of Shakespeare's plays collected by his fellow actors Heminge and Condell to preserve 'the memory of so worthy a friend'.

KING RICHARD II

In series with this book

Also edited by Dr J. H. Walter

HENRY V (Arden Shakespeare)

CHARLEMAGNE (Malone Society)

LAUNCHING OF THE MARY (Malone Society)

THE TRAGEDY OF

KING RICHARD II

Edited by
J. H. WALTER
M.A., PH.D.

Fellow of University College London
Formerly Headmaster
Minchenden School, Southgate

HEINEMANN EDUCATIONAL BOOKS
LONDON

Heinemann Educational Books Ltd

LONDON EDINBURGH MELBOURNE AUCKLAND TORONTO
HONG KONG SINGAPORE KUALA LUMPUR NEW DELHI
NAIROBI JOHANNESBURG LUSAKA IBADAN
KINGSTON

ISBN 0 435 19013 X

Published by
Heinemann Educational Books Ltd
48 Charles Street, London W1X 8AH
Printed and bound in Great Britain by
Morrison & Gibb Ltd, London and Edinburgh

CONTENTS

PREFACE

THE aim of this edition is to encourage pupils to study the play as a play, not as a novel or a narrative, but as a pattern of speech and movement creating an artistic whole. While it has been generally accepted that this approach stimulates and enlivens classroom work, it has more recently become clear that it is a most fruitful way of preparing for examinations. Reports issued by the University of Cambridge Local Examinations Syndicate call attention to this aspect in the work of examination candidates. The following comments are taken from an Advanced Level report:

'It will be seen that the best candidates are often those who show themselves conscious of the play as a made thing—usually, but by no means always, as a thing made for the theatre.' Again, 'And perhaps the most misunderstood aspect of Shakespeare is the part played by theatrical convention'.

The interleaved notes, therefore, contain, in addition to a gloss, interpretations of character, dialogue, and imagery, considered particularly from the point of view of a play. There are some suggestions for acting, for the most part simple pointers to avoid rigidity of interpretation and drawn up with an apron stage in mind. Some questions are interposed to provide topics for discussion or to assist in discrimination.

It is suggested that the play should be read through rapidly with as little comment as possible. On a second reading the notes should be used in detail, and appropriate sections of the Introduction might be read at the teacher's discretion.

It is hoped that this edition will enable the teacher to take his class more deeply into the play than the usual meagre allowance of time permits him to do; it is not an attempt to usurp his function.

I gratefully acknowledge help in preparing this edition from a considerable number of studies of *Richard II*. From them I give a list of books which may help the student:

N. Brooke, *Shakespeare's Early Tragedies*
G. Bullough, *Narrative and Dramatic Sources of Shakespeare* VII
Lily B. Campbell, *Shakespeare's Histories*
W. H. Clemen, *Shakespeare's Dramatic Art*
C. Leech and J. M. R. Margeson, *Shakespeare 1971*
T. McAlindon, *Shakespeare and Decorum*
R. Ornstein, *A Kingdom for a Stage*
I. Ribner, *The English History Play in the Age of Shakespeare*
E. W. Talbert, *The Problem of Order*
E. M. W. Tillyard, *Shakespeare's History Plays*
Glynne Wickham, *Shakespeare's Dramatic Heritage*.

The historical background may be studied in: F. R. H. Du Boulay and C. M. Barron, *The Reign of Richard II*, and Gervase Mathew, *The Court of Richard II*. M. M. Mahood, *Shakespeare's Wordplay*, reinforced by E. J. Dobson, *English Pronunciation, 1500–1700*, is very helpful over punning and quibbling.

I owe much to articles by R. D. Altick, J. Waters Bennett, P. Edwards, G. Lambrechts, L. Potter, M. Quinn, S. Snyder.

I am most grateful to my wife for help in discovering material, purging my errors, and disciplining my excesses, and to Jeanne Gooding for generously finding time to type copy.

REFERENCES

I have referred by author's or editor's name to the books or articles mentioned above and to the editions of the play by J. Dover Wilson (Cambridge), P. Ure (Arden), and S. Wells (New Penguin Shakespeare Series).

The following abbreviations are used: Q = *First Quarto* (1597); F = *First Folio* (1623).

Biblical quotations are from the *Bishops' Bible* (1575) with the spelling modernized. References to Shakespeare's plays not published in this series follow the line numbering of the Globe edition.

Preface

The text of this edition is based on that of the First Quarto (Q). A few readings from the First Folio (F) and from later Quartos have been preferred where they appear to correct the Q reading. The stage directions are adapted mainly from F, and a few further directions have been added to clarify the course of the action.

INTRODUCTION

I

THE first mention of *Richard II* is the entry in the *Stationers' Register* on 29 August 1597, licensing the publication of the play. In the same year a quarto edition (Q) was printed, probably from Shakespeare's 'foul papers' or a transcript of them. Resemblances between the play and Daniel's verse history, *The First Four Books of the Civil Wars* (1595), have been taken as evidence that Shakespeare borrowed from Daniel's poem. As Daniel borrowed from the play in his revised and enlarged edition of the *Civil Wars* (1609), it is argued that he would so have borrowed when writing his first edition in 1594, had the play been available to him on stage or in manuscript. On the other hand, as Ure notes, Daniel may have continued borrowing from the play as he had done in his first edition. This, however, would imply that the play was being staged as early as 1593–4, which seems unlikely. A suggestion that the lines, 'Our scene is altered from a serious thing, And now changed to "The Beggar and the King"' (V. iii. 78–9), are a glance at Chapman's play, *The Blind Beggar of Alexandria* (performed 1596) is very doubtful. It seems best to assume that the play was written in 1595.

The play was popular, for four more editions were printed before the First Folio edition (1623). The first three editions 1597, 1598 (two) did not contain the 'deposition scene' (IV. i. 154–317); the fourth edition (1608) printed an imperfect version of the scene based on a memorial report. The complete scene was printed in the Folio. It may be that the scene was suppressed by the authorities as dangerous political matter, or it may have been omitted by the printer, Simmes, who had been in serious trouble with authority before. There is little reason to doubt that the scene was included in performances of the play.

A letter dated 7 December 1595, from Sir Edward Hoby to Sir Robert Cecil inviting him to his house in Canon Row, Westminster, 'where as late as it shall please you a gate for your supper shall be open: and K. Richard present himself to your view', has been thought to refer to a private performance of the play. But 'K. Richard' could refer to another King Richard, or be the nickname of an acquaintance, or, as the letter is an invitation to supper, be a boar as a dish (i.e. Richard III).

There is less doubt about the performance given by Shakespeare's company at the Globe on Saturday, 7 February 1601, the eve of the Essex rebellion. Sir Charles Percy, Sir Jocelyn Percy, Lord Monteagle and other friends of the Earl of Essex asked the players to perform 'the play of the deposing and killing of King Richard the second', and 'promising to get them xls. more than their ordinary'. The players objected that 'the play of King Richard be so old and so long out of use as that they should have small or no company at it', a somewhat surprising statement in view of Queen Elizabeth's comment to Lambarde on the frequency of performances (see Appendix II). Finally they performed the play and at the subsequent trial of Essex were absolved from any blame. The only other record of a performance in Shakespeare's lifetime is one by the crew of William Keeling's ship, the *Dragon*, off Sierra Leone, on 30 September 1607.

II

ELIZABETH AND RICHARD II

Although Essex's followers used the play to incite their partisans, and Elizabeth herself was on occasions identified with Richard II (see Appendix II), it would be unwise to assume that the play was written as political propaganda, even though some believed that Essex was prepared to play Bolingbroke to Elizabeth's Richard II. Yet it would be perverse not to see in a play dealing with kingship, rebellion, regicide, and succession some reflection of sensitive topical issues.

Some contemporaries saw similarities between Elizabeth and Richard. Both it was held were influenced adversely by flatterers, both handed over monopolies and taxes to favourites, both did their utmost to avoid foreign wars, both were without heirs, both were the third generation of kings who had usurped the throne (Edward III and Henry VII) and on whom, according to the scriptures, God's vengeance would fall, both were victims of attacks from Roman Catholics (Archbishop Arundel intrigued to bring Bolingbroke from exile). Richard's deposition and death led to the hundred years of civil war. Was history going to repeat itself? His reign was the 'seed-bed for all the subsequent troubles for a century whichever way the particular moralist chose'. (M. Aston in *The Reign of Richard II*)

Elizabeth's position was precarious. In Protestant eyes she had been saved by God from martyrdom to fulfil an apocalyptic prophesy of a reformed Church; in an official Roman Catholic view she was a heretic, illegitimate, and without title to the crown. The attempt by the Northern Rebels (1569) to depose her resulted in an outpouring of tracts, pamphlets, and ballads, the reissue of an enlarged version of Foxe's *Acts and Monuments* (*Book of Martyrs*) (1570), and an enlarged *Book of Homilies* (1571) expressly condemning the sins of rebellion and disobedience to the monarch. This was to be read in churches nine times a year. Elizabeth faced further attempts at rebellion and assassination, papal encouragement to depose her, and attacks from a foreign enemy designed to dethrone her and convert the nation forcibly to Roman Catholicism. Abroad, events were not comforting. Two Protestant kings, William of Orange and Henri III of

France, had been murdered, and a third, Henri IV, saw Paris worth a mass. In the 1590s the succession to the throne was fiercely debated. Cardinal Allen and Robert Parsons argued (1592, 1594) that it was lawful to depose a monarch (i.e. Elizabeth), citing the deposition of Richard II as an example. Others fiercely rejected this view. Peter Wentworth's outspoken comments on the succession in the House of Commons landed him in jail in 1593. The approach of 1596, the year of Elizabeth's sixty-third birthday, her grand climacteric, when crises and changes were ominously foretold, was disturbing the astrologically minded— and the majority were. Elizabeth's life and the succession to the throne were not only of anxious concern to politicians and subject matter for professional polemicists, they were the themes of sermons and pamphlets presented to the common people.

III

SOME OPINIONS

The action throughout the play seems to develop through some force of its own, or by divine will.

W. H. Clemen, *Shakespeare 1971*

Richard, however, if he is meant to represent any single political principle, represents not a medieval king, but a Renaissance monarch with pretensions to a divine right and to a divine power which no medieval ruler could have claimed.

J. R. Elliott, Jr, *Renaissance Papers* (1965)

Richard II is a tragedy only if both protagonists and audience share the view that the king is a mystical being, a man of flesh and blood whose humanity is transfigured and exalted by his office. The sacramental notion of the king's person is so strongly and movingly presented that it is perverse to see it as a peculiar infatuation of Richard's.

P. Edwards, *Proceedings of the British Academy* (1970)

[*Richard II*] is the first play in which Shakespeare shows the ritualistic aspects of royalty, and it is his first working, in a formal way, of the concept of ceremony.

E. Z. Cohen, *Texas Studies in English*, 12 (1970–1)

Many critical studies of *Richard II* and a surprising number of productions, start from a curious assumption: that Shakespeare wrote, and asked his leading actor to star in, a long play dominated by a character whose main effect on the audience was to be one of boredom, embarrassment, or at best contemptuous pity.

Lois Potter, *Shakespeare Survey* 27

Thus *Richard II*, when its structure is examined, is seen to be not so much a tragedy in the classical sense as a political morality in the mediaeval sense.

Glynne Wickham, *Shakespeare's Dramatic Heritage*

Short perhaps in overt action, *Richard II* is rich in panoramas and peregrinations.

A. R. Humphrey, *Proceedings of the British Academy* (1968)

. . . in *Richard II*, we find a complex, far-reaching technique of preparation, which includes the use of premonitions, of prediction through omens and portents, imaginative anticipation, and ambivalent foreboding.

W. H. Clemen, *Shakespeare 1971*

Richard is presented struggling, but with an idea not with an antagonist.

M. Quinn, *Studies in Philology* (1959)

IV

GENERAL COMMENTS

Richard II is the first in historical order of two sequences of four plays, the whole cycle of eight plays covering the period from the usurpation of Henry IV to the union of York and Lancaster under Henry VII, the historical period treated in Hall's chronicle history *Union of the Two Noble and Illustre Families of Lancaster and York* (1548).

Richard's deposition was intensely interesting to Tudor historians who saw history as recurrent and therefore to be presented as examples to follow and errors to avoid. Shakespeare's treatment of the deposition naturally concentrates on the person of Richard, but it deals also with the complexities and contradictions of moral, religious, and political beliefs. Critics accordingly have propounded various interpretations of what the play is intended to portray: a political allegory for the instruction or warning of Elizabeth about the succession; disorder due to a youthful, headstrong, irresponsible king influenced by flatterers; incompatibility between the kingly function and the kingly person; the workings of Fortune's wheel whereby those of high degree were brought down to misery; an artistic recreation of a medieval tragedy; a discourse on the nature of a king and the divine order of society; the supplanting of an age of chivalry by the age of the nation-state.

It is inconceivable that Shakespeare would risk prison by attempting to instruct Elizabeth. Although Bolingbroke has Bushy and Green executed as flatterers who misled the King, and the Gardener talks of 'noisome weeds', there is no sign of their misleading Richard. Bolingbroke does not introduce an efficient nation-state, he restores the status quo, an essentially renaissance court although it has medieval elements. Richard certainly misconceives his kingship, and only when his own actions lead to his misfortune does he come to know himself. Finally, although the

nature of kingship and the social order play a part, they are not
treated didactically.

At first view or reading the play seems stiff, superficial, cold,
even awkward, restricted by formal rather than fused images,
by abundance of couplets together with situations of formal
ceremony, which in spite of the play's lyricism have suggested to
many the appearance of a Bordeaux tapestry. The stilted end-
stopped couplets, particularly in Act V, are reminiscent of the
conventional traditional verse produced in civic pageants such as
those by Anthony Mundy. Elizabeth's assertion that 'this tragedy',
believed to be Shakespeare's play, was acted forty times in streets
and houses (see Appendix II) suggests that it may well have been
presented in whole or in part in the style of a pageant. There is no
sub-plot, no comic character or episode—the Duchess of York's
plea for Aumerle is perhaps saved from being comedy by
Bolingbroke's light, general touch. Except for Richard's murder,
there is no violent action on the stage. All the male characters are
a little remote, they are not intimate with the audience, their
emotions are expressed almost formally in public. Apart from
Salisbury's brief prophecy (II. iv. 18–24), only Richard unpacks
his heart in soliloquy, and even that takes shape as a fantasy or
conceit.

The play is most intricately constructed with balanced and
antithetical scenes symmetrically arranged about the pivotal and
allegorical scene of the Queen and the Gardeners (III. iv). There
are parallels and balanced contrasts in the situations and responses
of Richard and Bolingbroke (as king). Both are faced with a
noble accused of treason, with a demand for trial by combat,
with actual treason, and both bear the accusation of murder. The
affairs of Gaunt and Bolingbroke are paralleled by those of York
and Aumerle. The three scenes in which the Queen is reduced to
despair (II. ii; III. iv; V. i) mirror and intensify the three scenes
of Richard's gradual fall, and both join in their despairing parting
(V. i). Some critics while acknowledging the symmetrical

balance, prefer to consider the play as a kind of symphony with four uneven parts: Richard in power (I. i–II. i. 223), Richard's loss of power (II. i. 224–III. i. 44), Richard's deposition (III. ii–V. i. 102), and Bolingbroke as king (V. ii–V. vi. 52). The play involves pageant and mystery-play elements, allegory and symbolism, scenic symmetries and parallels in a ceremonial and ritualistic treatment of sinful usurpation and the murder of a God-elected king. Continually there are overtones of divine providence and divine punishment. Two antithetical pictures enclose the movement of the play. At the beginning Richard is in majesty controlling the time of Bolingbroke's exile at a word, but threatened by the dead Gloucester. At the end Richard's kingdom is his prison, he is Bolingbroke's 'jack of the clock', and Bolingbroke is in majesty faced by the startling threat of Richard in his coffin.

Holinshed's very detailed description of Richard's coronation —the presentation of each item of the regalia, the sacred anointing, and the responses of the noblemen may have suggested to Shakespeare the ceremonial concept. Holinshed does not describe the coronation of any other monarch in this way. After Richard's return to England the symbolism of the coronation underlies the first two progressive steps of his fall, and is expressed openly in the powerful, climactic scene at Westminster.

By Barkloughly Castle (III. ii), he caresses the earth, calls it 'my earth', 'my gentle earth'; it is the living land of England over which part of the globe he shines as the sun. In spite of his assurance of divine assistance, gradually (by the defection or death of its defenders) he learns that his kingdom is lost. Only the earth that composes his body is left, and he is barren. In short Richard has lost all that is signified by the orb in his regalia.

At Flint Castle (III. iii) Shakespeare stresses Richard's appearance of majesty and authority, his pride, glory, and royal possessions. These he surrenders in submitting to Bolingbroke, longing for the holy life of a hermit in contempt of worldly vanities. Instead he suffers base humiliation, and the majesty and power signified by his sceptre (ll. 80, 151) passes to Bolingbroke.

Carlisle's searing denunciation of Bolingbroke's sinful intention to usurp the crown, and his prophecy of divine retribution (IV. i. 114–49), set the tone of the deposition scene. Richard's surrender of his kingship is a bitter coronation in reverse, a profane ironic parody, with the crown as the central symbol.

Holinshed's view of the deposition—'But the dejecting of the one, and advancing of the other, the providence of God is to be respected, and his secret will to be wondered at. For as in his hands standeth the donation of kingdoms, so likewise the dispersing of them consisteth in his pleasure'—is reflected in the play. Gaunt insists that vengeance must be left to God (I. ii. 37–41); Bolingbroke in reply to York's warning states that he will not oppose the will of heaven (III. iii. 18–19); York concludes, 'heaven hath a hand in these events, To whose high will we bound our calm contents' (V. ii. 37–8). The ceremonial tone and structure of the play keep decorum with the manifestation of the working of divine providence. In this way Shakespeare distanced the play, held it aloof from the danger of immediate topicality. At the same time he created in Richard a man divided in mind through whose human essence these things came about.

V

RICHARD

Richard has been interpreted as an irresponsible boy, a narcissist, a sensitive soul among brutal barons, an aesthete, a poseur, a poet manqué, a word-spinner, a sacramental man, a medieval martyr, 'a too quick despairer'; and qualified by such epithets as tyrannical, treacherous, unscrupulous, self-indulgent, feminine. Some recent stage presentations have introduced him as a sweet-eating fop, gossiping with lavishly dressed young favourites, or as nervous and uneasy, betraying by facial expression and stage business a guilty complicity in the murder of Gloucester. This last view should be rejected. Richard never mentions Gloucester. He does not admit guilt or show signs of being conscience-stricken, as Shakespeare's murderers frequently do, and Gaunt, though aware of Richard's responsibility for Gloucester's death, does not presume that it was wrong (I. ii. 39). For the most part these attributions are either incomplete or generalizations that do not match the particularity of the man.

Dover Wilson thinks that Richard is to be seen on two planes of vision, as a man and symbolically as a royal martyr. Others view him in the light of the legal concept of the king's two bodies oscillating between the body private and the body politic. There are marked fluctuations in Richard's attitudes and emotions, yet Shakespeare observes decorum, matching the 'pride of kingly sway' (IV. i. 205) with the 'kingly woe' (III. ii. 210) of abasement and despair. England for Richard becomes a living entity, an integral part of his identity as a king. In his pride he shows the majesty and greatness of Gaunt's vision; involved in his fall there is despair and death, 'The field of Golgotha and dead men's skulls' of Carlisle's prophecy, and the Elizabethan belief that the hundred years of civil wars began from the deposition of Richard. If, as seems probable, Shakespeare's cycle of history plays is inspired by the town cycles of mystery plays, then the correspondences hold. As the theme of the mystery plays was the preservation and forwarding of Christ's kingdom and the salvation of mankind, so in Shakespeare's cycle the theme is the preservation of royal England and of English men.

Richard dominates every scene in which he appears. As king or subject, in pride or despair, in submitting to Bolingbroke or in abdicating his throne, his intelligence and facility with words prescribe the course of the dialogue. His incisive comments expose the weaknesses of others, he probes their thoughts and motives, and characterizes their actions with sarcasm and accuracy that defies denial. At the same time he reveals himself, his blind self-deification, his narrow rationality, his anguish, and his flippancy.

The first scene presents Richard in the pride and ceremony of majesty, carrying out judicial functions with shrewdness and humanity. He points out the hypocrisy latent in one of the contestant's greetings, checks Bolingbroke's wild accusations by reminding him that the charge must be substantial if it is to hold against so worthy a man as Mowbray, and further deflates him with 'As he is but my father's brother's son'. His attempt to reconcile the two is not a sign of weakness but the proper course for a king, the physician of his country's health. Since the two are adamant on a point of honour, he directs that the dispute be submitted to God's judgment in trial by combat.

The mystic, divine nature of a king which the Elizabethans, including Elizabeth, believed in is touched on by Richard's reference to his 'sacred blood' and expanded by Gaunt who refuses to take arms against 'God's substitute, His deputy anointed in his sight', and who refuses to judge Richard as wrongfully having Gloucester killed. Richard's intervention in the duel is an assumption of God's office, since he had already placed the decision in God's hands. His blasphemous wish that God may expedite Gaunt's death reveals that for him God is an extension of his own personality to satisfy his impulses and desires. After his return from Ireland he boastfully misconceives his sacred immunity as 'The deputy elected by the Lord', who, 'for his Richard hath in heavenly pay A glorious angel', for every rebel Bolingbroke leads. At Flint Castle God, he claims, has not deposed him and will exact vengeance on his behalf on the rebels and smite their children with pestilence. Whether or not the symbol of the overthrow of Phaethon is meant to imply Richard's overthrow by divine power, from this point he makes no claim of special God-like authority; and in the following scene the allegory of the garden and the Fall of Man presents him as cast out by God. Hereafter although Carlisle fiercely defends his

THE WILTON DYPTYCH

Reproduced by courtesy of the Trustees, The National Gallery, London

divinity, Richard likens himself to the rejected Christ, man–god, surrounded by men who 'cry "All hail!" to me? So Judas did to Christ', who, 'with Pilate, wash your hands', and who, 'Have here delivered me to my sour cross'. Bolingbroke echoes the thought, mourning that 'blood should sprinkle me to make me grow'.

Richard's intense, though biased, piety with its angels and heavenly armies and analogues with Christ is not hypocrisy. Indeed, by some inspiration, or from some unidentified source, Shakespeare has drawn a figure not inconsistent with the deeply devout historical king—the king who apparently caused the symbolic Wilton Diptych (reproduced on pp. 16–17) to be painted with angelic figures wearing his white hart badge, and therefore his followers, while he adores the infant Christ, and whose virtues led to an appeal to him to form the chivalric order of the Passion of Christ. Scott-Giles, *Shakespeare's Heraldry* (p. 64), points out that Shakespeare may have been prompted by the double rank of angels bearing Richard's coat of arms in the roof of Westminster Hall, which Richard rebuilt, and the angel groups about his shield at the entrance.

By the time he leaves for Ireland Richard's 'unstooping firmness' of his 'upright soul' has become a mockery. He has acted on impulse rejecting the advice of his council, lost the love of the people and nobility, ruthlessly breached the right of succession by expropriating Gaunt's property, alienated himself from the land by the arrogant and insensitive exercise of absolute or, as he sees it, God-given power. It is from this pride that he plunges through grief to despair, foreshadowed by the mirror scene of the Queen's foreboding and despair, and reflected in the emblems of Phaethon and Adam both of whom offended through pride.

Richard's impulsive surrender to whims, Gaunt's 'rash fierce blaze', York's 'unstaid youth', his petulant self-will, denote emotional instability. His passionate greeting and invocation to

England on his return from Ireland is a fantasy misconceived by his belief in his divinity, and his grief at the loss of his inheritance. The chroniclers' insistence on Richard's child-like attitudes is perhaps reflected here. As the bad news continues to come, he struggles to preserve his identity as a king. He asserts his *character indelibilis*, the irreversible nature of his crowning, declares that his numinous presence will subdue the rebels, for angels will support him. But grief saps his will, 'time', he feels, 'hath set a blot upon my pride', and faced with the execution of his friends he speaks of the mortality of kings whose pomp and vain conceit is subject to death like ordinary mortals. Rejecting comfort he dismisses his troops, rejects defence, and abandons himself to 'that sweet way . . . to despair' to which deadly sin the proud deprived of hope succumb.

This pattern of descent is repeated when he encounters Northumberland and Bolingbroke. He maintains a royal presence against Northumberland, but this time he does not invoke God's immediate help, only prophesies that unborn generations will suffer punishment for the rebellion against God's steward. Compelled to retract Bolingbroke's exile he again despairs in his humiliation. For Elizabethans the ending of the sin of despair was either by repentance and a holy life or by suicide. Richard considers both. First, the anchorite's contempt for the world and search for obscurity. His conceit of the 'Two kinsmen digged their graves with weeping eyes' reveals that his imagination has overwhelmed his reason, a situation that in Elizabethan views could arise from emotional disturbance. Northumberland's comment 'Sorrow and grief of heart Makes him speak fondly like a frantic man', is just, yet Richard served him a flash of sharp irony, 'Will his majesty Give Richard leave to live till Richard die?', and brilliantly encapsulates his own position with the emblem of Phaethon. Even with his pride humbled Richard is capable of barbed sarcasm and mordant irony, agains which Bolingbroke has no reply.

In these two scenes Richard has been stripped first of the land, then of his personal authority, now in a third scene of similar structure he surrenders his crown and his sanctity. The climactic intensity of this ceremony is appropriately introduced by Carlisle's vehement accusation and warning, as from a bishop, a servant of God, 'best beseeming . . . to speak the truth'. Carlisle draws a parallel, 'this land be called The field of Golgotha and dead men's skulls', which anticipates the change in Richard to a Christ-like figure. Yet he likens himself to Judas. This is the third time he has been likened to a figure who in emblem literature fell from pride to despair or death [Phaethon (III. iii. 178), Adam (III. iv. 75–7)]. In spite of the formal ceremony Richard has demonstrated his reluctance to resign and that Bolingbroke has in fact seized the crown. The ritual deposition is not Richard's love of the theatrical, it is a necessary inverted ceremony that covers his torment as he gives 'The pride of kingly sway from out my heart'. In his agony of namelessness he calls for the mirror to seek the truth about himself. The emblem of pride he presents, the young man lavishly dressed holding up a mirror, is a last bitter irony, for the truth is that his vanity, his brittle glory, has gone, and with another bitter quibble he has been 'outfaced by Bolingbroke'. The breaking of the mirror symbolizes the complete destruction of kingly pride. He identified himself with an erroneous concept of his function, and that illusion destroyed, he becomes nothing.

His parting from his wife is a moving separation of lovers, revealing an acceptance of his position yet with the sharp perception that prophesies treachery by Northumberland. Similarly in York's account of Richard's patience in undergoing humiliation from the crowd in the entry into London, Shakespeare intended to rouse compassion for him.

In his meditation in prison he tries to come to terms with himself. Paradoxically he finds Christ's teaching contradictory. The rich young ruler and the little children, of whom is the kingdom of heaven, aptly and perhaps ironically relate to him. He is the rich young ruler who has given away his possession; he has been an irresponsible child but lacks the essential innocence implicit in the gospel—and his kingdom is not in heaven but in a prison. Even music, the emblem of harmony is disordered and reminds him of his own disordered time and the regularity of Bolingbroke's rule. Suddenly he becomes aware of human love in an 'all-hating world' confirmed by the loving visit from his former groom. At the threat of Exton's men Richard suddenly is no longer 'too careless patient', fights, and dies 'As full of valour as of royal blood'. His failure is his inability to reconcile free will with God's providence.

VI

BOLINGBROKE

Bolingbroke and Richard are balanced against each other, 'both are weighed' (III. iv. 84) in Fortune's scales, and like Fortune's buckets one is 'dancing in the air', the other 'down, unseen, and full of water' (IV. i. 185–6). The play itself is divided: the first part shows Richard dominant, the second part shows Bolingbroke achieving complete control. In the opening scenes Bolingbroke is aggressive. The charge he brings against Mowbray is 'boisterous', his temperament is 'high-stomached', he is full of ire, and his claim to be the avenger of his uncle Gloucester's death provokes Richard's inference of his arrogance, 'How high a pitch his resolution soars'. Yet he is depicted as a man determined vigorously to right wrongs and to restore order. Even in his angry exchanges of insult with Mowbray his insistence on pride of birth and honour as conferring both integrity and duties implies sincerity, though the element of a blood feud cannot be ruled out however much Gaunt denies that 'ancient malice' is involved.

At Coventry Shakespeare gives him an emotional and

prestigious leave-taking, stressing both his relationship to the king and his proud descent by contrast with Mowbray's quiet, isolated dignity. He receives the sentence of exile with restraint, but is anxious to establish the truth of his charge by urging Mowbray to confess his guilt. It is only in conversation with his father that he shows bitterness, rejecting Gaunt's profitable advice given at some cost to himself, and reveals an unimaginative acceptance of the realities of exile. He consistently employs practical, realistic notions. He finally consoles himself by asserting that his birthright of an Englishman cannot be removed.

Throughout Act I Shakespeare introduces occasional prophetic ironies as if he is giving the audience a nudge to remind them of the course of history. While the audience may enjoy the prospect of a confident absolute ruler heading unawares for disaster, Shakespeare may intend a further irony through Richard's words: 'How high a pitch his resolution soars', 'nay [were he] my kingdom's heir', and in comment on Bolingbroke's courtesy towards the common people, ' "Thanks, my countrymen, my loving friends", As were our England in reversion his, And he our subjects' next degree in hope', Richard in fact confirms unconsciously Bolingbroke's king-like qualities some of which he himself lacks. At the same time he suspects Bolingbroke's motives and is envious of his popularity. Indeed, is Bolingbroke sincere in his affability towards the common people or astutely ingratiating himself with them?

Bolingbroke's gift as a conversationalist, a much prized attribute, is highly praised by Northumberland on the way to Berkeley Castle, but it is not apparent. Northumberland cannot be absolved from gross flattery. Bolingbroke responds lightly to Northumberland, and is adequately gracious to Harry Percy and other supporters with cautiously conditional promises of rewards.

Confronted by York he is not without subtlety. He is punctilious over the names Herford and Lancaster, invites York to be impartial, but immediately invokes him as a substitute father to exercise nepotism, and completes the appeal to family ties by drawing a parallel between himself and Aumerle, York's son. Again he claims that he comes to right injustice and to remove the King's companions who exploit the country. Assuming supreme judicial powers and justifying his action by accusing Bushy and Green of misleading the King, injuring his own status and inheritance, he orders them to be executed without trial. It is significant that both men make no confession of guilt, but condemn Bolingbroke. In response to York's warning of heavenly judgment Bolingbroke promises not to oppose the will of heaven, reaffirms his allegiance and loyalty to Richard, and apparently sees with awe Richard's appearance on the castle walls. The negotiations are conducted through the mediation of Northumberland as if Shakespeare is using him as a scapegoat to lighten the burden of oath-breaking and treason from Bolingbroke, and attract to himself the dislike of Richard and the audience. In the base-court it is Richard's feelings that are exposed, not Bolingbroke's whose brief direct remarks leave Richard scope. Bolingbroke is never alone to voice his inmost thoughts and feelings through a soliloquy, he takes advantage of the situations opportunely made for him by others.

In London Bolingbroke assumes the office of king in dealing with the accusations against Aumerle and the subsequent challenges; and on news that Richard relinquishes the throne to him, announces his assumption to it. He ignores Carlisle's rightful protest and approves of, or acquiesces in, his arrest, though later he pardons him. Again it is Northumberland who arrests Carlisle. Bolingbroke sends for Richard, but again Northumberland takes over after the single sentences of Bolingbroke leading to the ceremonial deposition, in which verbal exchanges he is outmanoeuvred by Richard. Out of pity or impatience he stops Northumberland's insistence on the reading of the charges. He sees the mirror episode merely superficially as a practical man, and his low-key brevity is perhaps devised by Shakespeare to give Richard's emotion full exposure.

Blest by the common people Bolingbroke reflects uneasily on his dissolute and absent son, acts coolly and genially with Aumerle's conspiracy, exercising the royal divine prerogative of mercy both to Aumerle and to Carlisle. At last he gives way to open emotion protesting that his soul is 'full of woe That blood should sprinkle me to make me grow', and he promises repentance and expiation.

There remains something enigmatic about him. Is he king by a divine thrusting on, is he an unscrupulous opportunist, or a man of destiny? He is a usurper, but Shakespeare has given a more favourable view of him than the chroniclers do.

VII

MOWBRAY

Mowbray, by comparison with Bolingbroke in I. i, iii, is a more controlled and dignified figure. His position is difficult, but he defends himself frankly, avoiding the involvement of a family feud implicit in Bolingbroke's intention to avenge Gloucester's death. He denies the deed, which he ought to have carried out, and points out that his offence against Gaunt has been pardoned. He claims that unless he is allowed to challenge the slanders, his honour and good name will be irretrievably lost, and he would prefer death. Bolingbroke also stands upon the honour he would lose if he withdrew the charges since this, he alleges, would imply cowardice. Bolingbroke's farewells in preparation for the duel are more emotional and confident of success than Mowbray's claim that his 'dancing soul doth celebrate This feast of battle with mine adversary' (I. iii. 91–2), his wish for a long life for his fellows, and the chivalric, 'As gentle and as jocund as to jest Go I to fight. Truth hath a quiet breast' (I. iii. 95–6). His exile is a shock to him; he had expected, 'A dearer merit, not so deep a maim', from Richard. It may be that Richard was expelling Mowbray as a scapegoat for Gloucester's death, even as Bolingbroke expelled Sir Piers Exton. Bolingbroke later is still prepared to pursue the matter of Gloucester's death by recalling Mowbray, but news of Mowbray's death prevents it. Is the point of Carlisle's tribute to Mowbray's Christian life and death to suggest that Mowbray was innocent and virtuous all along, or that he repented and expiated his sins, or implicitly to contrast Bolingbroke's guilt with his glory? There is nothing like this in Shakespeare's source. Again, is it the spark that anticipates Bolingbroke's urgency to go on a crusade to atone for Richard's death?

VIII

GAUNT

Gaunt, the battle-tried statesman, is Shakespeare's creation, there is nothing like his character in the chronicle histories. His loyalty and integrity are shown in his refusal, unlike his son, to pursue vengeance for the murder of his brother Gloucester, and in his concurrence in the exiling of his son. His grief he subdues and tries to rally the spirits of the resentful Bolingbroke by encouraging him to use his imagination to make a virtue of necessity and to ease his sorrows by treating his exile as a light affliction. On his death-bed, assuring himself through proverbial wisdom that Richard will at last heed his warnings, with inspired recollection he speaks of England's former magnificence now reduced to a 'pelting farm'. His bitter puns on his name when Richard arrives establish his anxious care for England, care that should have been the task of Richard. Bluntly he condemns Richard's succumbing to flatterers, and with prophetic irony sees Richard deposing himself. On Richard's threat to have him executed he challenges him to continue shedding family blood and live afterwards with shame and a sick conscience. 'Old John of Gaunt, time-honoured

Lancaster', as becomes so famous a warrior, is tough and uncompromising, a visionary and a patriot.

IX

YORK

York is first heard as a critic of Richard's love of vanities and imperviousness to counsel. Yet he is a conciliator. He cautions Gaunt to deal mildly with Richard, and begs Richard to realize Gaunt's love for him. He is roused by Richard's unjust seizure of Gaunt's property to contrast Richard unfavourably with his father, the Black Prince, and he points out that by seizing Bolingbroke's inheritance he is breaking the rights of succession to which he himself owes his kingdom. It is part of his loyalty and mildness that he suffers Richard to sweep aside his protest and make him Lord Governor of England while Richard is in Ireland. That he is inadequate in the hour of need is not his fault, he is faced with revolting nobles and commons. Richard's close friends disperse, and York has to do what he can 'to order these affairs Thus disorderly' from his own resources. Moreover, his duty to his king, and his conscience concerned for a kinsman wronged, leave him with a divided mind. He puts a bold face on matters when he meets Bolingbroke, but his inability to oppose him is obvious; and after Bolingbroke's assurances of his intention solely to claim his own, he decides to 'remain as neuter', an impossible standpoint to maintain. Thereafter he supports Bolingbroke, but he warns him not to go too far. Later, he offers Bolingbroke the crown, declaring that Richard willingly resigns the office. York's conduct is logical: he serves the new king and fiercely denounces his own son for treason. The usurpation has brought his loyalty and that of his son into absurd conflict, and perhaps this much-tried man may have compassion in response to his last words 'Pardonne-moi'.

X

NORTHUMBERLAND

Northumberland leads the conspiracy against Richard in England. At his first appearance he rouses the others' sympathy for Bolingbroke and fear for their own safety, and declares that Richard's rule is leading to disaster. He informs them of Bolingbroke's invasion fleet and urges the others to join Bolingbroke. His flattery of Bolingbroke is fulsome, and he it is who supports him in persuading York that Bolingbroke has sworn an oath that he comes 'But for his own'. Again he is Bolingbroke's emissary to Richard, and he assures Richard that Bolingbroke has sworn by all he holds sacred that he merely comes for his inheritance. If this is granted he will lay down his arms. It is he who torments Richard by insisting that he read the articles of accusation. He is again Bolingbroke's agent in separating Richard from his Queen during which episode Richard foretells his treason against Bolingbroke. Shakespeare may be anticipating his next plays *1* and *2 Henry IV* or merely the events of history, but it seems certain that Northumberland is used to attract to himself the blame and audience's ill-feeling for what is Bolingbroke's crime. Bolingbroke during his confrontation with Richard speaks no hostile or contemptuous word—that is left to Northumberland.

XI

OTHER CHARACTERS

The Duchess of Gloucester, the Duchess of York, and Queen Isabel all serve the same dramatic function, to rouse up pity and to plead for some action or decision. They make chorus-like comments on the situation and lament, but only the Duchess of York is successful in her plea. Shakespeare presents the Queen as a mature woman (in history she was eleven years old) amplifying the course of Richard's fall with significance and passion. She has three important appearances, and in each the pattern of the scene reflects the three scenes in which Richard is gradually bereft of kingship. In the first, like Portia in *Julius Cæsar*, she is filled with foreboding, then in the imagery of childbirth laments the unnatural birth of news of rebellion and gives way to despair. In the second, the garden scene, the threat of deposition is to her expulsion from the Garden of Eden, and she curses the Gardener's plants that they may wither, an image of barrenness born of despair. Finally, she and Richard are brought together as lovers. She, remembering his beauty, is distressed at his humility and pleads in vain that she may remain with him. In violation of the marriage service bidding, 'Those whom God hath joined together, let no man put asunder', she is put asunder from her king and husband just as he was forced from his kingship, and both are left despairing.

XII

THEMES, IMAGES, AND DEVICES OF STYLE

Pointing and amplifying the structure of the play, sometimes integrating with it, sometimes illuminating it with a figure of speech, are certain themes, concepts repeated by direct word or by image and allusion, together forming a whole dramatic impression.

England might almost be a protagonist in the play. In different forms—earth, land, kingdom, realm, little world, garden, country —it occupies the thoughts of all the main characters. Some important aspects of the theme are presented in the first act: 'kingdom's heir' (I. i. 116), and 'England in reversion his' (I. iv. 35); the shedding of English blood on the earth (I. iii. 124–5); 'farm our royal realm' (I. iv. 45)—all of which are repeated later. Gaunt's inspired vision of England as 'This other Eden', 'this little world', 'This blessed plot' (II. i. 40–57) is the past set up as a measure for the present 'pelting farm' (II. i. 60), 'sleeping

28

England' (II. i. 77), a land let 'by lease' (II. i. 110) which others
see as 'declining' (II. i. 240) and broken winged (II. i. 292). After
Bolingbroke's landing, to York the land is 'woeful' (II. ii. 99)
and needs underpropping (II. ii. 82), but Bolingbroke sees it
infested with 'caterpillars of the commonwealth' (II. iii. 165) to
be weeded out. Richard, in spite of Gaunt's accusation that he
has become landlord of England, feels movingly as a mother for
her child; to him she is wounded by horses' hoofs, and he
expresses an intimate and mystical bond with her (III. ii. 8–26).
He knows that he has lost his kingdom (III. ii. 95). Again he fears
injury to England, that dead sons of England, 'Shall ill become
the flower of England's face' (III. iii. 97), and, 'bedew Her
pastures' grass with faithful English blood' (III. iii. 99–100). He
would exchange his 'large kingdom for a little grave' (III. iii. 153).
Then in the garden scene England is treated allegorically as an
untended, disordered garden transformed by the Queen's
anguished words into Eden and 'a second Fall of cursed man'
(III. iv. 76). The fear that 'blood of English shall manure the
ground' (IV. i. 137) is voiced again by Carlisle, and the 'cursed
earth' will become, 'The field of Golgotha and dead men's
skulls' (IV. i. 144). The Queen condemns the 'rebellious earth'
(V. i. 5); Richard, too, the 'all-hating world' (V. v. 66) though
he experiences a touch of love. England is left with 'A deed of
slander . . . Upon . . . all this famous land' (V. vi. 35–6) for 'the
King's blood [hath] stained the King's own land' (V. v. 110).

The religious element in Richard's kingship has been discussed
elsewhere, but the theme spreads throughout and enriches the
play. Blood, guilt, and vengeance are linked with allusions to
Cain and Abel (I. i. 103–6, V. vi. 43); Adam, Eve, the serpent,
Eden, the Fall of Man are reflected in Richard's deposing (III. iv.
73–6); God is the protector of widows (I. ii. 43; *Psalms*, lxviii. 5)
and the sole avenger of wrongs (I. ii. 6–8, 40–1; *Rom.*, xii. 19),
Christ's betrayal, trial, and crucifixion and its participants are
linked with Richard (IV. i. 170, 238–41, 143–4). Verbal echoes

occur: 'blotted from the book of life' (I. iii. 202; *Rev.*, iii. 5. See also IV. i. 235). Christ's teaching is quoted, 'house against this house' (IV. i. 145; *Mark*, iii. 25) and expressions derived from his rebuke, 'Suffer little children to come unto me, and forbid them not: for unto such belongeth the kingdom of God' and the nearby comment on the rich young ruler, 'For it is easier for a camel to go through a needle's eye, than for a rich man to enter into the kingdom of God' (V. v. 15–17; *Luke*, xviii. 16, 25). The Christian life is variously included. 'Sacred', 'sacrament', 'pilgrimage' occur more frequently than in other Shakespearian plays. The withdrawn life of hermit and palmer is exquisitely described (III. iii. 147–54), and the heavenly reward of an 'immortal title' (I. i. 24) or a 'new world's crown' (V. i. 24) for a holy life is referred to, together with the felicity of a pilgrimage to the 'sepulchre . . . Of the world's ransom, blessed Mary's son' (II. i. 55–6). Mowbray, after fighting on a crusade dies, giving 'his pure soul unto his captain Christ, Under whose colours he had fought so long' (IV. i. 99–100).

Richard's solicitude lest English blood should be shed on English soil is part of a theme that is widespread and varied. The word blood is used in its normal sense of vital fluid, for royal descent, for preserving inheritance of family qualities, for guilt, courage, sacrificial offering, vengeance, and stimulating growth. The contention of Bolingbroke and Mowbray demands blood-letting to settle it (I. i. 51, 149, 153, 172, 194). So does Bolingbroke's intention to avenge Gloucester's death (I. i. 103–8) as both inherit the blood which Richard (I. i. 119) and the Duchess of Gloucester (I. ii. 12, 17) consider 'sacred'. The Duchess's image of Edward III's seven sons 'as seven vials of his sacred blood' contains overtones. The 'seven vials of blood' image was known from *Rev.*, xv–xvii where the seven angels emptied from them the wrath of God upon the world through calamities and disease. That from the seven sons of Edward III came the disastrous Wars of the Roses is a possible inference from this image. Blood soils, stains, showers on, bedrenches, manures English earth. Bolingbroke confesses 'my soul is full of woe That blood should sprinkle me to make me grow' (V. vi. 45–6), and he undertakes to go on pilgrimage 'to the Holy Land To wash this blood off from my guilty hand' (V. vi. 49–50). Bolingbroke uses Pilate's image here as he does earlier (III. i. 4–5; see IV. i. 238–41) to cleanse himself from guilt.

References to water and washing are closely linked with tears (IV. i. 206; V. i. 10) and hence with weeping, sorrow, grief, woe. There are far more such expressions in *Richard II* than in any other Shakespearian play. Apart from the three women characters who mourn, Richard himself is shown as a man of sorrows and acquainted with grief. If we think he laments excessively, it is worth bearing in mind the principle of decorum and recalling Richard's, 'there I'll pine away. A king, woe's slave, shall kingly woe obey' (III. ii. 209–10), and later, 'O that I were as great As is my grief (III. iii. 136–7). With his tears Richard ritually washes away the balm of his anointing (IV. i. 206), something he had previously declared 'Not all the water in the rough rude sea' could accomplish (III. ii. 54–5).

On three occasions water or weeping is associated with the sun. Salisbury, after the departure of the Welsh soldiers sighs over Richard's future, 'Thy sun sets weeping in the lowly west, Witnessing storms to come, woe, and unrest' (II. iv. 21–2). Bolingbroke the invader, like the rivers that 'drown their shores . . . So high above his limits swells the rage' (III. ii. 107–9) now anticipating his meeting with Richard at Flint Castle says, 'Be he the fire, I'll be the yielding water' (III. iii. 58); finally Richard, having surrendered his office, realizes that he is nameless and wishes, 'O that I were a mockery king of snow, Standing before the sun of Bolingbroke, To melt myself away in water-drops!' (IV. i. 259–61). The two have changed elemental images: Richard, the sun king, has become through grief the yielding water, Bolingbroke is now the sun in Richard's place.

Throughout the earlier part of the play the sun is Richard's symbol. Shakespeare may have known that Richard had two emblem badges of the sun, but the analogy between the king and the sun was a general one. Salisbury anticipates Richard's fall in his sunset image, but Richard's allusion to the fall of Phaethon, son of Phoebus the sun god, as he descends the castle walls is vivid symbolic linking of image and action (III. iii. 178). After this Richard looks in vain in the mirror for 'the face That like the sun did make beholders wink?' (IV. i. 282–3).

Richard, seeking with Isabel by 'holy lives' to win 'a new world's crown', adds, 'Which our profane hours here have thrown down' (V. i. 24–5). Later he confesses, 'I wasted time, and now doth time waste me' (V. v. 49). The theme of time pervades the play. Richard by contrast with 'time-honoured Gaunt' is a spendthrift of time, both of his own time and of others', as Bolingbroke says bitterly, 'How long a time lies in one little word' (I. iii. 213). Yet after Bolingbroke has broken his 'time', Salisbury longs to 'bid time return' for Richard (III. ii. 69), but it has already set a blot upon his pride (III. ii. 81). Thence listening to 'time broke in a disordered string' (V. v. 46) he is brought to consider his own misuse of time so that now he is wasted by time, a mere clock to record the hours by the sighs of his own grief, the measure of Bolingbroke's joy. Though he does not 'redeem the time', yet he perceives true time and with that an awareness of the harmony of love, before his 'untimely bier' (V. vi. 52). Other themes have been suggested: tongue and word, sour and sweet, honour.

Images and devices of style aim at emphasizing a thought, clarifying a point, amplifying a mood, stressing an emotion, and pointing an original and striking association of ideas.

The images of *Richard II* are for the most part explicit and not fused. The two contestants are 'deaf as the sea, hasty as fire', and Bolingbroke's comparison, 'Since the more fair and crystal is the sky, The uglier seem the clouds that in it fly' (I. i. 41–2) has a naïveté perhaps emphasized by the stilted couplet. Occasionally an image is extended. Thus the seven vials of Edward's blood and the seven branches are elaborated over eleven lines (I. ii. 11–21); and Mowbray's fears for his 'native English' over fifteen lines, moving from a useless musical instrument to an imprisoned tongue, leading to a bitter quibble on 'sentence' (I. iii. 159–73). There are antitheses: 'Things sweet to taste prove in digestion sour' (I. iii. 236); the word-order of antimetabole: 'As the last taste of sweets, is sweetest last' (II. i. 13); and lists of 'sentences' or wise sayings (II. i. 34–9). There are memorable pieces of description such as Gaunt's England (II. i. 40–58) and specific images tautly developed such as the 'antic death' (III. ii. 160–70). Some images allude to emblems and carry the overtones and associations of symbol or allegory: Phaethon (III. iii. 178), buckets and well (IV. i. 183–8), mirror (IV. i. 275–88).

Devices such as anaphora, the repetition of the same word at the beginning of successive clauses (III. iii. 143–53, IV. i. 206–9) are used for emphasis. Contraries are juxtaposed 'Ay, no; no, ay' (IV. i. 200), 'Which art possessed now to depose thyself' (II. i. 108); and a number of negative words beginning with 'un' have been observed: 'undeaf' (II. i. 16), 'unhappied' (III. i. 10), 'unkinged' (V. v. 37), 'unkiss' (V. i. 74).

The Elizabethans regarded the pun as an elegant deployment of wit not a cheap joke, and it was also expressive of a wide range of emotions from jest to the stretched nerve. There were four varieties: a word which when repeated shifts its meaning—'craftsmen', 'craft' (I. iv. 28), 'rue', 'rue' (III. iv. 105–6); a word having at the same time two different meanings—'breath' (I. iii. 173), 'nicely' (II. i. 84), 'mortal' (III. ii. 161), 'antic' (III. ii. 162), 'journeyman' (I. iii. 274); words repeated which are similar in sound or spelling—'Ay', 'I' (IV. i. 200); a word returned with a new meaning as a riposte—'faced', 'outfaced' (IV. i. 284–5), 'Gaunt' (II. i. 74), 'high', 'highway' (I. iv. 3–4), 'name' (II. i. 86–7).

XIII

VERSE

The play is written in verse except for V. v. 100–1 which is prose, though it has been suggested that the omission of 'My Lord', perhaps caught from two lines earlier, or the substitution of 'late' for 'lately', would leave two lines of blank verse. Dover Wilson has argued that some loose ends over Exton's appearance (in Q), some factual errors (V. vi. 8 note), some inadequate couplets (V. vi. 7–10), indifferent rhymes (V. vi. 41–4) and what appear to be couplets buried in blank verse, indicate that Shakespeare was working on an old play, and that particularly 'Shakespeare in a hurry or a mood of lassitude or indifference' left 'the bones of the old play . . . sticking through in almost every scene'. It does not seem necessary to invent an old play to account for the discrepancies of Shakespeare's draft. Memorial contamination by a transcriber, and revision or completion by someone other than Shakespeare, are possibilities. Shakespeare, too, it must be admitted was capable of very poor verse. Even so, the rhymes 'liege', 'beseech' (V. iii. 90–1), and 'labour', 'favour' (V. vi. 41–2) are poor by any standards.

Couplets are distributed throughout the play. Where the tone of the scene is lighter or conversational, as in II. ii, iii, iv, there are only couplets that mark the conclusion of a speech or scene. Elsewhere they add weight to a proverb (II. i. 7–8; III. iii. 202–3) or an edge to a pointed remark—often a concluding couplet as well (III. iii. 194–5; IV. i. 316–17). Where emotion is stressed, couplets are used sometimes in clusters (III. iv. 96–101); or a whole passage of tense emotion will be arranged in couplets (V. i. 81–102; V. iii. 74–135; V. vi. 31–52; I. i. 160–95). Other uses are to emphasize an image (I.iii. 221–4), or a wish (IV. i. 174–5, 213–20). An interesting group occurs in the deposition scene. Richard invites Bolingbroke to 'seize the crown', draws the analogy of the buckets in the well, and relates it to his grief.

At this point couplets are introduced (l. 187) and continue, except for one line, while Richard talks of his cares until he states that he will resign the crown (l. 201). The ceremonial deposing is in blank verse but couplets begin again when Richard calls on God to pardon oathbreakers.

The nature of I. i, the formal, ceremonial situation in the royal presence, curbs the utterances of the characters. Then blank verse has a rigidity that channels 'the bitter clamour of two eager tongues' into prescribed expressions without correlative action. Similarly in I. iii the formal declarations, the legal phrasing, control the verse form. Richard's verse is on the whole terse and very much to the point, with more compact metaphors by comparison with the combatants' looser similes and comparisons. Gaunt, as befits a wise counsellor, orders his advice of Boling-broke with logistic skill of propositions, premise, and a threefold amplification. Bolingbroke retorts with a series of rhetorical questions in end-stopped lines. The texture of verse in I. iv is conversational, approaching prose, indeed but that Shakespeare does occasionally use a six-footed line, 'Marry would the word "farewell" have lengthened hours', might be taken as prose. Gaunt's famous speech (II. i. 31–68) with its prelude of 'sentences' or proverbs is skilfully constructed and embellished with allitera-tion, consonant grouping, and effective metaphors. Most effective is the contrasting 'That' (l. 65) after the emphasis on 'This'. Later in the scene Gaunt's style is both fluent and flexible.

By contrast York's verse in II. i is not so effective. In ll. 163–85 it is as if York is talking to himself, indeed the point is made in Richard's response, 'Why uncle, what's the matter?'. His argu-ment is not well organized even in his next speech (ll. 186–208) where he does make an important point.

After Richard's return from Ireland his speech reflects his change in mood. It is discursive, fancifully explorative of images, sometimes at length (III. ii. 36–53, 160–70). Again, he poses a question and with highly imaginative invention provides the answer (III. iii. 143–70) in discursive narrative style. Carlisle speaks with considerable eloquence and force (IV. i. 91–100, 114–49) in a precisely ordered attack on Bolingbroke's usurpation.

Richard's confrontation with Bolingbroke in IV. i provokes him into a flexible, varied style with extremely effective irony. Then after the ceremonial deposition his retort to Northumberland is in verse of power and authority. Throughout Richard's speeches the device of anaphora is frequent as is his use of the terse aphoristic phrase, and deft alliteration: 'the unseen grief That swells with silence in the tortured soul' (IV. i. 296–7).

After Bolingbroke's inflationary style in I. i and iii, he becomes reticent and factual. To York he states his claim in plain, direct style, and in similar style he condemns Bushy and Green (III. i. 1–30). He says very little in the deposition scene. He merely issues orders, keeps Richard to the point over the resignation, and makes a common-sense comment on the breaking of the mirror.

KING RICHARD II

CHARACTERS

KING RICHARD THE SECOND
JOHN OF GAUNT, DUKE OF LANCASTER } uncles to the king
EDMUND OF LANGLEY, DUKE OF YORK
HENRY BOLINGBROKE, DUKE OF HERFORD, son of John of Gaunt; afterwards King Henry IV
THOMAS MOWBRAY, DUKE OF NORFOLK
DUKE OF AUMERLE, son of Duke of York
DUKE OF SURREY
EARL OF SALISBURY
LORD BERKELEY
SIR JOHN BUSHY
SIR WILLIAM BAGOT } King Richard's servants
SIR HENRY GREEN
EARL OF NORTHUMBERLAND
HENRY PERCY, his son
LORD ROSS
LORD WILLOUGHBY
LORD FITZWATER
BISHOP OF CARLISLE
ABBOT OF WESTMINSTER
LORD MARSHAL
SIR STEPHEN SCROOP
SIR PIERS EXTON
WELSH CAPTAIN

Characters

QUEEN ISABEL, King Richard's wife
DUCHESS OF GLOUCESTER
DUCHESS OF YORK
Ladies attending the Queen
Gardeners, Keeper of the prison, Groom of the stable to King
Richard
Lords, Heralds, Officers, Soldiers, Attendants

SCENE: *England and Wales*

There is no act and scene division in Q. The act and scene division in this text is that of F except for V. iv, which the Folio incorporates with V. iii.

The events represented here take place at Windsor Castle.

A full ceremonial entry. What grouping is appropriate and where should Richard be enthroned? (See note to l. 186.)

1   *Old . . . Lancaster.* Gaunt represents a former age of military triumphs and chivalric custom. The contrast between that age and Richard's reign is a theme that gives depth and spaciousness as well as setting up a standard of judgment. *time-honoured.* Contrast Richard's 'true time broke' (V. v. 48).

2   *band,* bond, pledge.

3   *Herford.* So pronounced in the play for Hereford.

4   *boisterous,* violent, unruly. The word is condemnatory as often in Shakespeare.

5   *our.* The royal plural. *leisure,* lack of leisure. *hear,* i.e. hear and judge. Does this speech hint at the character of Bolingbroke in 'bold', 'boisterous'; and of Richard in 'leisure'?

8   *sounded,* questioned.

9   *on ancient malice,* out of long-held hatred. Again the glance back to the past.

10   *worthily,* in good faith.

11   *known ground,* well-founded evidence.

12   *As . . . argument,* as closely as I could examine him about the matter.

13   *apparent,* manifest.

14   *inveterate,* (a) long-standing, deep-rooted, (b) embittered.

18–19   *High . . . fire.* Is the couplet an emphatic description or a cue for entry?

18   *High-stomached,* proud, haughty.

19   *deaf . . . sea,* i.e. to entreaty or command.

ACT ONE

SCENE ONE

Enter KING RICHARD, JOHN OF GAUNT, *with other nobles and attendants*

KING RICHARD: Old John of Gaunt, time-honoured Lancaster,
  Hast thou according to thy oath and band
  Brought hither Henry Herford, thy bold son,
  Here to make good the boisterous late appeal,
  Which then our leisure would not let us hear,
  Against the Duke of Norfolk, Thomas Mowbray?
JOHN OF GAUNT: I have, my liege.
KING RICHARD: Tell me moreover, hast thou sounded him
  If he appeal the Duke on ancient malice,
  Or worthily as a good subject should   10
  On some known ground of treachery in him?
JOHN OF GAUNT: As near as I could sift him on that argument,
  On some apparent danger seen in him
  Aimed at your highness, no inveterate malice.
KING RICHARD: Then call them to our presence;
                                        [*Exit Attendant*
                                        face to face,
  And frowning brow to brow, ourselves will hear
  The accuser and the accused freely speak.
  High-stomached are they both and full of ire,
  In rage deaf as the sea, hasty as fire.

20–1   *Many . . . liege.* Did Shakespeare assume that his audience would know of Bolingbroke's usurpation and appreciate this as irony?

22–4   *Each . . . crown.* The paradoxical conceit marks the more accomplished courtier.

23   *hap,* fortune.

24   *Add . . . crown,* make your crown an immortal one in heaven.

25–7   *We . . . treason.* Is there any hint of duplicity or should Richard be played straight?

26   *you,* for which you.

28   *object,* bring forward as evidence.

30–3   *First . . . hate.* Bolingbroke asserts on oath the integrity of his motive, but see ll. 98–108 which imply a desire for vengeance.

30   *record,* witness.

32   *Tendering,* (a) having proper regard for, (b) offering my liability for.

34   *appellant,* accuser.

36   *greeting,* words, speech.

38   *Or . . . heaven,* or if slain in trial by combat my immortal soul shall answer for it before God's judgment seat.

39   *miscreant,* treacherous villain,

40   *Too good,* i.e. by nobility of birth or rank.

41–6   *Since . . . prove.* What is the purpose of these end-stopped rhymes: formality, emphasis, peroration, to mark epigrammatic style? Some consider them to be traces of an earlier play. Bolingbroke has made no specific charge.

41–2   *Since . . . fly.* For similar view of clouds see III. iii. 65–7, 86–7.

43   *aggravate the note,* add to the disgrace.

46   *right-drawn,* drawn in a rightful cause.

47   *Let . . . zeal,* do not let the restraint of my speech put my fervent loyalty in question.

49   *eager,* sharp, bitter.

51   *cooled,* i.e. shed in a 'trial' by combat.

Enter BOLINGBROKE *and* MOWBRAY

BOLINGBROKE: Many years of happy days befall   20
  My gracious sovereign, my most loving liege.
MOWBRAY: Each day still better other's happiness
  Until the heavens, envying earth's good hap,
  Add an immortal title to your crown.
KING RICHARD: We thank you both, yet one but flatters us,
  As well appeareth by the cause you come,
  Namely, to appeal each other of high treason.
  Cousin of Herford, what dost thou object
  Against the Duke of Norfolk, Thomas Mowbray?
BOLINGBROKE: First, heaven be the record to my speech,   30
  In the devotion of a subject's love,
  Tendering the precious safety of my prince,
  And free from other misbegotten hate,
  Come I appellant to this princely presence.
  Now Thomas Mowbray do I turn to thee,
  And mark my greeting well; for what I speak
  My body shall make good upon this earth,
  Or my divine soul answer it in heaven.
  Thou art a traitor and a miscreant,
  Too good to be so, and too bad to live,   40
  Since the more fair and crystal is the sky,
  The uglier seem the clouds that in it fly.
  Once more, the more to aggravate the note,
  With a foul traitor's name stuff I thy throat,
  And wish—so please my sovereign—ere I move,
  What my tongue speaks my right-drawn sword may prove.
MOWBRAY: Let not my cold words here accuse my zeal.
  'Tis not the trial of a woman's war,
  The bitter clamour of two eager tongues,
  Can arbitrate this cause betwixt us twain.   50
  The blood is hot that must be cooled for this.

52   *tame patience.* Patience is not a virtue to those like Bolingbroke, Duchess of Gloucester, or Mowbray who would invoke their honour or urge revenge. Contrast Gaunt and York. The frequent occurrence of 'patience' and 'patient' in the play has been noted.

54   *reverence of,* respect due to. *curbs.* 'reins', 'spurs', 'post', extend the image.

55   *From . . . spurs,* from relaxing the reins and urging with spurs.

56   *post,* hasten.

57   *terms of treason,* i.e. 'traitor' and 'miscreant'.

58–9   *Setting . . . liege.* Bolingbroke was grandson of Edward III and Richard's cousin.

60   *spit at,* speak contemptuously of.

63   *tied,* bound, obliged.

65   *inhabitable,* not habitable, uninhabitable—where a fight to the death could take place without interference. A common expression. See ll. 93–4 and IV. i. 74; *Macbeth,* III. iv. 104.

67   *this,* his sword, or perhaps his denial in the next line.

68   *hopes,* i.e. of heaven.

69   *gage,* glove. Holinshed records that hoods were thrown down.

70–1   *Disclaiming . . . royalty.* Any irony in this renunciation?

72   *except,* take exception to, protest against. Some interpret 'set aside', and refer to l. 58, but the 'setting aside' was not an act of fear, it was Mowbray's claim to be swayed by reverence.

74   *pawn,* pledge.

77   *thou . . . devise,* any worse plots that you can contrive.

79   *gently,* i.e. with ennobling touch, honourably.

80   *in . . . degree,* in any honourable manner. 'Degree' may glance back at the difference in rank (ll. 58–9, 70–1), and the phrase= on any level.

81   *Or . . . trial,* or in trial by combat according to the code of chivalry.

Yet can I not of such tame patience boast
As to be hushed, and naught at all to say.
First the fair reverence of your highness curbs me
From giving reins and spurs to my free speech,
Which else would post until it had returned
These terms of treason doubled down his throat.
Setting aside his high blood's royalty,
And let him be no kinsman to my liege,
I do defy him, and I spit at him, 60
Call him a slanderous coward, and a villain,
Which to maintain I would allow him odds,
And meet him, were I tied to run afoot
Even to the frozen ridges of the Alps,
Or any other ground inhabitable
Where ever Englishman durst set his foot.
Meantime, let this defend my loyalty—
By all my hopes most falsely doth he lie.

BOLINGBROKE: Pale trembling coward, there I throw my gage,
Disclaiming here the kindred of the King, 70
And lay aside my high blood's royalty,
Which fear, not reverence, makes thee to except.
If guilty dread have left thee so much strength
As to take up mine honour's pawn, then stoop.
By that, and all the rites of knighthood else,
Will I make good against thee, arm to arm,
What I have spoke, or thou canst worse devise.

MOWBRAY: I take it up, and by that sword I swear
Which gently laid my knighthood on my shoulder,
I'll answer thee in any fair degree, 80
Or chivalrous design of knightly trial;

45

82   *light*, alight, dismount.

      So far the dispute seems mainly personal (ll. 18–19). What importance has the stress on Bolingbroke's royal blood and kinship with Richard (ll. 54–9, 70–1)?

85–6   *inherit . . . of*, put us in possession of. Has 'inherit us' overtones of irony?

87   *Look what*, whatever.

89   *lendings*, advances of money to soldiers when regular payments are not possible.

90   *lewd*, base, improper.

91   *injurious*, pernicious, unjust.

95   *for . . . years*, i.e. since the rebellion of the commons under Wat Tyler, 1381.

96   *Complotted*, plotted with others.

97   *Fetch*, derive. *head*, source.

100   *he . . . death*. Thomas of Woodstock, Duke of Gloucester, uncle of Richard and Bolingbroke, was put to death while a prisoner in charge of Mowbray at Calais. It was generally believed that Mowbray had the murder carried out at Richard's instigation. See IV. i. 2–13 for a different version.

101   *Suggest*, incite. *soon-believing*, easily convinced.

102   *consequently*, subsequently, afterwards.

104–6 *Which . . . chastisement*. See *Genesis*, iv. 4–10. Abel's offerings of the firstlings of his sheep was acceptable to God, his brother Cain's offerings were not. Out of jealousy Cain killed Abel. God said to Cain, 'the voice of thy brother's blood crieth unto me from the ground', and he cursed Cain and drove him away as a fugitive. Bolingbroke, however, has overlooked the sevenfold vengeance to be taken on anyone who slew Cain (*Genesis*, iv. 15).

106   *rough*, severe.

106–8 *To . . . spent*. Bolingbroke reassumes his royal descent (l. 71) and arrogates to himself the right to dispense justice—or vengeance.

And when I mount, alive may I not light,
If I be traitor or unjustly fight!
KING RICHARD: What doth our cousin lay to Mowbray's
    charge?
It must be great that can inherit us
So much as of a thought of ill in him.
BOLINGBROKE: Look what I speak, my life shall prove it
    true:
That Mowbray hath received eight thousand nobles
In name of lendings for your highness' soldiers,
The which he hath detained for lewd employments,   90
Like a false traitor, and injurious villain.
Besides I say, and will in battle prove
Or here or elsewhere to the furthest verge
That ever was surveyed by English eye,
That all the treasons for these eighteen years
Complotted and contrived in this land
Fetch from false Mowbray their first head and spring.
Further I say, and further will maintain
Upon his bad life to make all this good,
That he did plot the Duke of Gloucester's death,   100
Suggest his soon-believing adversaries,
And consequently like a traitor coward,
Sluiced out his innocent soul through streams of blood,
Which blood, like sacrificing Abel's, cries
Even from the tongueless caverns of the earth
To me for justice and rough chastisement.
And by the glorious worth of my descent,
This arm shall do it, or this life be spent.

109   *How ... soars.* Perhaps an allusion to the falcon badge of Lancaster. A suggestion that Bolingbroke presumes to exceed his natural position in the divine order. *pitch.* The highest point of flight gained by a falcon in order to stoop (swoop down) on its prey.

113   *slander ... blood,* disgracer of the royal descent.

116   *my kingdom's heir.* Is this ironic?

118   *sceptre's awe,* reverence due to my sceptre.

120   *partialize,* sway, bias.

124–5   *as ... liest.* An extension of a common expression. See l. 44.

126   *that ... had,* that sum of money I received. *Calais.* Pronounced and spelled 'Callice'.

128   *by consent.* Holinshed does not record that Richard agreed to the retention of the money.

130   *Upon ... account,* for the balance of heavy expenses. *dear,* (a) costly, (b)='dire', heavy, serious.

131   *Since ... queen.* In 1395 Mowbray went to France to negotiate the marriage between Richard and his second wife, Isabel, daughter of Charles VI. Richard himself 'fetched' Isabel in the following year.

132–4   *For ... case.* According to Holinshed Richard ordered Mowbray, then Governor of Calais, to have Gloucester put to death secretly. Mowbray delayed until Richard threatened to execute him if the order was not carried out quickly.

133   *I ... not,* i.e. Mowbray did not kill Gloucester with his own hands, but employed others.

134   *Neglected ... case,* i.e. by delaying Gloucester's death.

135–7   *For ... life.* So Holinshed, but nothing further is known.

140   *exactly,* expressly, in every point.

KING RICHARD: How high a pitch his resolution soars.
  Thomas of Norfolk, what sayst thou to this?   110
MOWBRAY: O let my sovereign turn away his face,
  And bid his ears a little while be deaf,
  Till I have told this slander of his blood,
  How God and good men hate so foul a liar.
KING RICHARD: Mowbray, impartial are our eyes and ears.
  Were he my brother, nay, my kingdom's heir,
  As he is but my father's brother's son,
  Now by my sceptre's awe I make a vow,
  Such neighbour nearness to our sacred blood
  Should nothing privilege him, nor partialize   120
  The unstooping firmness of my upright soul.
  He is our subject, Mowbray, so art thou.
  Free speech and fearless I to thee allow.
MOWBRAY: Then Bolingbroke as low as to thy heart
  Through the false passage of thy throat thou liest.
  Three parts of that receipt I had for Calais
  Disbursed I duly to his highness' soldiers;
  The other part reserved I by consent,
  For that my sovereign liege was in my debt
  Upon remainder of a dear account   130
  Since last I went to France to fetch his queen.
  Now swallow down that lie. For Gloucester's death,
  I slew him not, but to my own disgrace
  Neglected my sworn duty in that case.
  For you my noble lord of Lancaster,
  The honourable father to my foe,
  Once did I lay an ambush for your life,
  A trespass that doth vex my grieved soul.
  But ere I last received the sacrament,
  I did confess it, and exactly begged   140
  Your grace's pardon; and I hope I had it.

142   *appealed*, with which I am charged.

144   *recreant*, faithless. *degenerate*, ignoble.

146   *interchangeably*, in exchange for his.
147   *overweening*, presumptuous.

149   *Even . . . bosom*, i.e. by shedding his very heart's blood.
150   *In haste whereof*, to hasten which.

153   *purge . . . blood*, drain off this anger without bloodshed. *purge*, cleanse the body, empty the bowels. *choler*, (a) anger, (b) bile. *letting blood*, (a) drawing off blood from a vein, (b) bloodshed.
      Choler was one of the four humours created by digestion in the stomach, and which passed into the blood. Excess of it in the blood could be controlled therefore either by purging or bloodletting.

154   *though no physician*. A king was in fact frequently described as the physician of his people. See *Macbeth*, V. ii. 27–9.
156   *Forget, forgive*. Proverbial jingle. *conclude*, settle the matter.
157   *Our . . . bleed*. Doctors claimed to determine the best times for bleeding a patient, and favourable periods were also noted in the almanacs of the period.

164   *boot*, remedy.

167   *The . . . owes*, my duty as a subject places my life in your hands.
167–9 *but . . . have*, but my good name which lives on, although I am dead, on my tombstone I will not submit to suffer dishonour.

170   *impeached*, accused of treason. *baffled*, publicly defamed. In early times a perjured knight or his shield was suspended upside down in public.

172–3 *his . . . Which*, the heart blood of him who.

This is my fault. As for the rest appealed,
It issues from the rancour of a villain,
A recreant and most degenerate traitor,
Which in myself I boldly will defend,
And interchangeably hurl down my gage
Upon this overweening traitor's foot,
To prove myself a loyal gentleman,
Even in the best blood chambered in his bosom.
In haste whereof most heartily I pray   150
Your highness to assign our trial day.

KING RICHARD: Wrath-kindled gentlemen, be ruled by me,
Let's purge this choler without letting blood.
This we prescribe, though no physician;
Deep malice makes too deep incision.
Forget, forgive, conclude, and be agreed.
Our doctors say this is no month to bleed.
Good uncle, let this end where it begun.
We'll calm the Duke of Norfolk, you your son.   159

JOHN OF GAUNT: To be a make-peace shall become my age.
Throw down, my son, the Duke of Norfolk's gage.

KING RICHARD: And Norfolk, throw down his.

JOHN OF GAUNT: When, Harry, when?
Obedience bids I should not bid again.

KING RICHARD: Norfolk, throw down we bid, there is no
boot.

MOWBRAY: Myself I throw, dread sovereign, at thy foot.
My life thou shalt command, but not my shame;
The one my duty owes, but my fair name,
Despite of death that lives upon my grave,
To dark dishonour's use thou shalt not have.
I am disgraced, impeached, and baffled here,   170
Pierced to the soul with slander's venomed spear,
The which no balm can cure but his heart-blood
Which breathed this poison.

174   *lions . . . tame*. The heraldic lions rampant were part of Richard's royal coat of arms. The heraldic leopard, a lion in any other posture, was Mowbray's crest (Scott-Giles, *Shakespeare's Heraldry*, p. 75).

175   *but . . . spots*. Proverbial (*Jer.*, xiii. 23). *spots*, (a) coat, nature, (b) stains of shame.

177–   *The . . . done*. Iago similarly praises 'reputation' (*Othello*, III. iii.
83   155–61).

177   *mortal times*, men's lives. *afford*, accomplish.

182   *in one*, as one.

184   *try*, prove.

186   *throw up*. Perhaps on to the dais where Richard is enthroned. O.E.D. does not record the meaning 'surrender', 'relinquish', until 1678, though it would be apt here. F reads 'throw down'.

188   *crest-fallen*, humiliated. Perhaps a glance at 'crest' as a symbol of honour.

189   *beggar-fear*, base cowardice. *impeach my height*, shame my high birth.

190   *outdared*, (a) exceeded in daring, (b) daunted, over-awed. *dastard*, coward.

191   *such feeble wrong*, wrong of speaking so feebly (Wells), or, uttering a wrong like a feeble man.

192   *sound . . . parle*, utter so ignoble a speech. The image is military implying a request for a truce, usually to discuss terms for surrender.

192–3 *my . . . fear*, my teeth will bite off my tongue if it utters this cowardly retraction.

193   *motive*, instrument, i.e. tongue. Such an incident is used in Kyd's *Spanish Tragedy* (1587), IV. iv. 193–4.

195   s. d. in F only. According to Elizabethan stage convention Gaunt, who enters at the beginning of I. ii, should not be on stage at the end of I. i. There seems to be no other reason for his departure here.

199   *Saint Lambert's Day*, 17 September.

200   *arbitrate*, decide.

201   *swelling difference*, inflamed quarrel.

KING RICHARD: Rage must be withstood.
  Give me his gage; lions make leopards tame.
MOWBRAY: Yea, but not change his spots. Take but my shame,
  And I resign my gage. My dear dear lord,
  The purest treasure mortal times afford
  Is spotless reputation; that away,
  Men are but gilded loam, or painted clay.
  A jewel in a ten-times barred-up chest   180
  Is a bold spirit in a loyal breast.
  Mine honour is my life, both grow in one,
  Take honour from me, and my life is done.
  Then, dear my liege, mine honour let me try;
  In that I live, and for that will I die.
KING RICHARD: Cousin, throw up your gage; do you begin.
BOLINGBROKE: O God defend my soul from such deep sin.
  Shall I seem crest-fallen in my father's sight?
  Or with pale beggar-fear impeach my height
  Before this outdared dastard? Ere my tongue   190
  Shall wound my honour with such feeble wrong,
  Or sound so base a parle, my teeth shall tear
  The slavish motive of recanting fear,
  And spit it bleeding in his high disgrace
  Where shame doth harbour, even in Mowbray's face.
                          [Exit John of Gaunt
KING RICHARD: We were not born to sue, but to command,
  Which since we cannot do to make you friends,
  Be ready as your lives shall answer it,
  At Coventry upon Saint Lambert's Day.
  There shall your swords and lances arbitrate   200
  The swelling difference of your settled hate.

202   *atone*, reconcile.

203   *Justice . . . chivalry*, God's justice will determine the victor in a chivalric combat.

204   *Marshal*, the Duke of Surrey. The Marshal's duty was to see that the rules of combat were obeyed and the trial conducted in an orderly manner.

      Is Richard—an effeminate, sweet-eating fop, joking with his extravagantly dressed favourites; nervous and anxious lest his guilt over Gloucester's death should be exposed; a 'pale Galilean' type of martyr figure among robust violent nobles; a striker of attitudes; a shrewd practical man; a reasonable humanitarian mediator; every inch a king?

      Themes that reappear are—the mystic, sacramental nature of kingship, honour, breed (blood), a subject's obedience to his king, the importance of oath-taking, reference to past history.

Gaunt's House

There is nothing in the accepted sources that provides matter for this scene; it is of Shakespeare's devising.

1–8   The biblically knowledgeable Elizabethan audience may have been reminded of the parable of the unjust judge and the widow (*Luke*, xviii. 2–5):

1   *the . . . blood*, the fact that I was brother to Thomas of Woodstock, Duke of Gloucester. *Woodstock's*. F 'Glouster's', perhaps to be consistent with the use of the name Gloucester throughout the rest of the play.

2   *solicit*, weigh with, persuade. *exclaims*, outcries.

4–5   *since . . . correct*, since authority to punish the murder rests with the man (i.e. Richard) responsible for the crime which we ourselves cannot remedy.

6   *Put . . . quarrel*, let us submit our cause.

6–8   *will . . . heads*. The imagery is biblical. See *Psalms*, xi. 6.

Since we cannot atone you, we shall see
Justice design the victor's chivalry.
Lord Marshal, command our officers-at-arms
Be ready to direct these home alarms.   [*Exeunt*

SCENE TWO

Enter JOHN OF GAUNT *with the* DUCHESS OF GLOUCESTER

JOHN OF GAUNT: Alas, the part I had in Woodstock's blood
   Doth more solicit me than your exclaims
   To stir against the butchers of his life.
   But since correction lieth in those hands
   Which made the fault that we cannot correct,
   Put we our quarrel to the will of heaven;
   Who, when they see the hours ripe on earth,
   Will rain hot vengeance on offenders' heads.
DUCHESS OF GLOUCESTER: Finds brotherhood in thee no
      sharper spur?
   Hath love in thy old blood no living fire?   10
   Edward's seven sons, whereof thyself art one,

12–20　*Were . . . faded.* The symbolism of the two linked images inten-
sifies the significance of the passage. *seven.* In biblical concept a
mystical, perfect number.

12　*seven vials.* Doubtfully an echo of the 'seven vials' of *Rev.*, xv. 7
and xvi, hinting at the wrath of God, which may follow the
pouring out of the contents of the vials.

13　*branches . . . root.* The pictured genealogical tree with the founder
of a family as its root, and his descendants as branches growing
above was extremely popular among the Elizabethans. It may
derive from the Jesse windows in medieval churches, themselves
based on *Isaiah*, xi. 1, 'And there shall come forth a rod out of
the stem of Jesse, and a branch shall grow out of his roots', and
the image of Christ as the vine, *John*, xv.

14–15　*Some . . . cut.* Two sons died young, Edward, the Black Prince,
died in 1376, Lionel, Duke of Clarence, in 1368. Thomas of
Woodstock, Duke of Gloucester, was murdered in 1397.

15　*branches . . . cut.* The 'destinies' in classical myth, Clotho, Lachesis,
and Antropos, wove the web of each person's life and cut off the
completed pattern. Here that allusion is fused with the figure of
the cut branch, a commonplace indicating premature, violent
death. See *3 Henry VI*, II. vi. 46–51.

17　*blood,* (a) breed, (b) blood, the vital fluid.

21　*envy's,* hatred's. *axe.* English versions record that Gloucester was
smothered; only a French version, *Chronique de la Trahison et
Mort de Richard Deux*, states that Gloucester was beheaded.
Shakespeare may merely be sustaining the imagery of blood.

23　*mettle,* essence, stuff, intrinsic quality. *self,* same.

28　*model,* image, copy.

31　*naked,* unguarded (i.e. against murderers).

33　*mean,* common, ordinary, i.e. not noblemen.

37–8　*for . . . sight,* i.e. Richard. The view of Richard as God's deputy
is repeated in III. ii. 57; IV. i. 126. Elizabethan commonplaces
were that the king was God's deputy, that it was impious to rebel
against him, and that vengeance was to be left solely to God. All
these derive from passages in the Bible. See *Rom.*, xiii. 1–7;
1 Sam., xxvi. 9; *Rom.*, xii. 19.

39　*his,* Gloucester's.

43　*To . . . defence.* See *Psalms*, lxviii. 5; *1 Tim.*, v. 5.

Were as seven vials of his sacred blood,
Or seven fair branches springing from one root.
Some of those seven are dried by nature's course,
Some of those branches by the destinies cut;
But Thomas my dear lord, my life, my Gloucester,
One vial full of Edward's sacred blood,
One flourishing branch of his most royal root,
Is cracked, and all the precious liquor spilt,
Is hacked down, and his summer leaves all faded,   20
By envy's hand, and murder's bloody axe.
Ah Gaunt, his blood was thine, that bed, that womb,
That mettle, that self mould, that fashioned thee
Made him a man; and though thou livest and breathest,
Yet art thou slain in him. Thou dost consent
In some large measure to thy father's death
In that thou seest thy wretched brother die,
Who was the model of thy father's life.
Call it not patience, Gaunt, it is despair.
In suffering thus thy brother to be slaughtered,   30
Thou showest the naked pathway to thy life,
Teaching stern murder how to butcher thee.
That which in mean men we entitle patience
Is pale cold cowardice in noble breasts.
What shall I say? To safeguard thine own life,
The best way is to venge my Gloucester's death.
JOHN OF GAUNT: God's is the quarrel—for God's substitute,
His deputy anointed in his sight,
Hath caused his death; the which if wrongfully,
Let heaven revenge, for I may never lift   40
An angry arm against his minister.
DUCHESS OF GLOUCESTER: Where then, alas, may I
    complain myself?
JOHN OF GAUNT: To God the widow's champion and defence.

46   *cousin*, kinsman. *fell*, cruel.

49   *if . . . career*, if Mowbray is not overthrown at the first charge.

53   *caitiff recreant*, base traitor.
54   *sometimes*, sometime, i.e. she who was once your brother's wife.

58–9   *Grief . . . weight*, grief rebounds like a ball, but because of its heaviness not because of its hollowness. The Duchess excuses her reluctance to go.

62   *York*, i.e. the Duke of York.

66   *Pleshey*, Gloucester's house near Chelmsford in Essex.

68   *lodgings*, rooms. *unfurnished walls*, walls from which the tapestry had been removed, or an empty house.
69   *Unpeopled offices*, empty servants' quarters.

DUCHESS OF GLOUCESTER: Why then I will. Farewell old
    Gaunt.
  Thou goest to Coventry, there to behold
  Our cousin Herford and fell Mowbray fight.
  O sit my husband's wrongs on Herford's spear
  That it may enter butcher Mowbray's breast.
  Or if misfortune miss the first career,
  Be Mowbray's sins so heavy in his bosom   50
  That they may break his foaming courser's back
  And throw the rider headlong in the lists,
  A caitiff recreant to my cousin Herford.
  Farewell old Gaunt, thy sometimes brother's wife,
  With her companion grief, must end her life.
JOHN OF GAUNT: Sister farewell, I must to Coventry.
  As much good stay with thee as go with me.
DUCHESS OF GLOUCESTER: Yet one word more. Grief
    boundeth where it falls,
  Not with the empty hollowness, but weight.
  I take my leave before I have begun,   60
  For sorrow ends not when it seemeth done.
  Commend me to thy brother Edmund York.
  Lo this is all. Nay yet depart not so,
  Though this be all, do not so quickly go.
  I shall remember more. Bid him—ah, what?—
  With all good speed at Pleshey visit me.
  Alack and what shall good old York there see
  But empty lodgings and unfurnished walls,
  Unpeopled offices, untrodden stones?

70   *hear* Q. Some copies of Q have 'cheere'. But 'hear there' balances 'there see' (l. 67).

The scene does not further the action, but it identifies Richard as the instigator of Gloucester's murder, propounds further the theme of the divine right of kings, reveals the influence of past events and of blood relationships. It presents Gaunt's integrity as a wise, elderly counsellor, and rouses pity for the desolation of the Duchess. There are marked religious tones and biblical echoes, and the first of several portrayals of grief.

Coventry

Initially the scene is fully ceremonial with legal formalities of identification, declaration of intent, statement of the matter in contention, and justification by oath-taking. After Richard's intervention (l. 118) the tone changes to theatricality.

2   *at all points*, completely, in all parts. *enter in*. The stage represents the lists or field of combat.

3   *sprightfully*, spiritedly.

4   *Stays . . . trumpet*. The correct procedure was for the appellant to enter first, and the defendant, summoned by the herald's trumpet, to enter afterwards. Shakespeare changes the order perhaps to render it easier to link Bolingbroke's 'appeal' with his extended leave-taking and to delineate more of his character.

9   *orderly*, according to the rules.

10   *swear . . . cause*. A knight about to engage in trial by combat was required to declare on oath that his cause was just.

11   *In . . . art*. Identification had to be made under most solemn conditions because the knight's face might be concealed by the visor.

18   *defend*, forbid.

And what hear there for welcome but my groans?   70
Therefore commend me. Let him not come there
To seek out sorrow that dwells everywhere.
Desolate, desolate will I hence and die.
The last leave of thee takes my weeping eye.   *[Exeunt*

SCENE THREE

Enter the LORD MARSHAL *and the* DUKE OF AUMERLE

LORD MARSHAL: My Lord Aumerle, is Harry Herford armed?
AUMERLE: Yea, at all points, and longs to enter in.
LORD MARSHAL: The Duke of Norfolk, sprightfully and bold,
  Stays but the summons of the appellant's trumpet.
AUMERLE: Why then, the champions are prepared, and stay
  For nothing but his majesty's approach.

  The trumpets sound and the KING *enters with his nobles. When
  they are set, enter* MOWBRAY, *in arms defendant, and a* HERALD

KING RICHARD: Marshal, demand of yonder champion
  The cause of his arrival here in arms;
  Ask him his name, and orderly proceed
  To swear him in the justice of his cause.   10
LORD MARSHAL [*to Mowbray*]: In God's name and the King's,
    say who thou art,
  And why thou comest thus knightly clad in arms,
  Against what man thou comest, and what thy quarrel.
  Speak truly on thy knighthood and thy oath,
  And so defend thee heaven and thy valour.
MOWBRAY: My name is Thomas Mowbray Duke of Norfolk,
  Who hither come engaged by my oath—
  Which God defend a knight should violate—

20   *my succeeding issue.* Some prefer F 'his' for 'my' on the grounds that it follows a customary form of declaration of loyalty. But Q 'my' is retained since if Mowbray's guilt is confirmed by his defeat, his descendants would be in danger of attainder, also it parallels 'me' in l. 24. *issue*, children.

21   *appeals*, accuses.

25   *truly*, in a true cause.

       s.d. Some add a stage direction for Mowbray to sit down on a chair. Ure notes that what Holinshed referred to as a 'chair' was a small pavilion, but that it is not known whether a Shakespearian performance staged such a property.

26   *ask* Q, F. Some prefer 'demand of' to regularize the metre and to parallel 'demand of' in l. 7.

28   *plated . . . war*, clad in plate-armour.

30   *Depose him*, swear him.

45   *fair designs*, honourable enterprises.

Both to defend my loyalty and truth
To God, my King, and my succeeding issue,   20
Against the Duke of Herford that appeals me;
And by the grace of God, and this mine arm,
To prove him, in defending of myself,
A traitor to my God, my King, and me.
And as I truly fight, defend me heaven.

The trumpets sound. Enter BOLINGBROKE, *appellant,*
in armour, and a HERALD

KING RICHARD: Marshal, ask yonder knight in arms
Both who he is, and why he cometh hither
Thus plated in habiliments of war;
And formally according to our law,
Depose him in the justice of his cause.   30
LORD MARSHAL: What is thy name? And wherefore comest
   thou hither
Before King Richard in his royal lists?
Against whom comest thou? And what's thy quarrel?
Speak like a true knight, so defend thee heaven.
BOLINGBROKE: Harry of Herford, Lancaster, and Derby
Am I, who ready here do stand in arms
To prove by God's grace, and my body's valour
In lists, on Thomas Mowbray Duke of Norfolk,
That he is a traitor foul and dangerous
To God of heaven, King Richard, and to me.   40
And as I truly fight, defend me heaven.
LORD MARSHAL: On pain of death, no person be so bold
Or daring-hardy as to touch the lists,
Except the Marshal, and such officers
Appointed to direct these fair designs.
BOLINGBROKE: Lord Marshal, let me kiss my sovereign's hand,
And bow my knee before his majesty;
For Mowbray and myself are like two men

50–1   *Then . . . friends.* The leave-takings in Holinshed took place earlier; they would not be part of a formal trial by combat. Shakespeare places them here to increase the emotional effect and enlarge character.

54–8   *We . . . dead.* Is this—hypocrisy, favouritism, irresponsibility, impulsive sympathy?

55   *as*, in so far as.

57–8   *which . . . dead*, i.e. because Bolingbroke would by his death have demonstrated his guilt.

59–60   *O . . . spear*, if I am disgraced by being killed by Mowbray, let no nobleman debase a tear by weeping for me.

61–2   *As . . . bird.* See I. i. 109.

66   *cheerly*, in good spirits.

67–8   *as . . . sweet.* English banquets customarily ended with sweetmeats. See II. i. 13.

67   *regreet*, greet again.

68   *daintiest*, (a) tastiest, (b) most precious.

70   *regenerate*, reborn.

73   *proof*, toughness, impenetrability.

74   *steel*, harden.

75   *waxen coat*, i.e. armour as if it were wax.

76   *furbish*, (a) polish (armour), (b) add lustre to.

77   *haviour*, behaviour.

79   *execution*, action.

81   *amazing*, stunning. *casque*, helmet.

That vow a long and weary pilgrimage.
Then let us take a ceremonious leave,   50
And loving farewell of our several friends.
LORD MARSHAL: The appellant in all duty greets your highness,
    And craves to kiss your hand, and take his leave.
KING RICHARD: We will descend and fold him in our arms.
    Cousin of Herford, as thy cause is right,
    So be thy fortune in this royal fight.
    Farewell, my blood, which if today thou shed,
    Lament we may, but not revenge thee dead.
BOLINGBROKE: O let no noble eye profane a tear
    For me, if I be gored with Mowbray's spear.   60
    As confident as is the falcon's flight
    Against a bird, do I with Mowbray fight.
    [*To Lord Marshal*] My loving lord, I take my leave of you;
    Of you, my noble cousin, Lord Aumerle;
    Not sick, although I have to do with death,
    But lusty, young, and cheerly drawing breath.
    Lo, as at English feasts, so I regreet
    The daintiest last, to make the end most sweet.
    [*To John of Gaunt*]
    O thou, the earthly author of my blood,
    Whose youthful spirit in me regenerate   70
    Doth with a two-fold vigour lift me up
    To reach at victory above my head,
    Add proof unto mine armour with thy prayers,
    And with thy blessings steel my lance's point
    That it may enter Mowbray's waxen coat,
    And furbish new the name of John o' Gaunt,
    Even in the lusty haviour of his son.
JOHN OF GAUNT: God in thy good cause make thee prosperous.
    Be swift like lightning in the execution,
    And let thy blows, doubly redoubled,   80
    Fall like amazing thunder on the casque

65

84   *Mine . . . thrive*, may my innocence and the aid of St George give me success.

90   *uncontrolled enfranchisement*, freedom from control.

92   *feast*, festival.

95   *to jest*, to take part in a pageant or masque, to sport.

97–8   *securely . . . eye*, I see honour and courage confidently reposing in your eye. Dover Wilson takes it to mean that Richard trusts Mowbray's loyalty implicitly and that he will not betray him.

101   *Receive thy lance*. The Marshal has measured the lances to see that they are of equal length.

102   *Strong . . . hope*. See *Psalms*, lxi. 3, 'and a strong tower from the enemy'.

106   *On . . . be*, under penalty of being.

112   *approve*, prove.

Of thy adverse pernicious enemy.
Rouse up thy youthful blood, be valiant, and live.
BOLINGBROKE: Mine innocence and Saint George to thrive.
MOWBRAY: However God or fortune cast my lot,
  There lives or dies true to King Richard's throne,
  A loyal, just, and upright gentleman.
  Never did captive with a freer heart
  Cast off his chains of bondage, and embrace
  His golden uncontrolled enfranchisement   90
  More than my dancing soul doth celebrate
  This feast of battle with mine adversary.
  Most mighty liege, and my companion peers,
  Take from my mouth the wish of happy years.
  As gentle and as jocund as to jest
  Go I to fight. Truth hath a quiet breast.
KING RICHARD: Farewell, my lord, securely I espy
  Virtue with valour couched in thine eye.
  Order the trial, Marshal, and begin.
LORD MARSHAL: Harry of Herford, Lancaster, and Derby, 100
  Receive thy lance, and God defend the right.
BOLINGBROKE: Strong as a tower in hope, I cry 'Amen.'
LORD MARSHAL: Go bear this lance to Thomas Duke of
  Norfolk.
FIRST HERALD: Harry of Herford, Lancaster, and Derby
  Stands here for God, his sovereign, and himself,
  On pain to be found false and recreant,
  To prove the Duke of Norfolk, Thomas Mowbray,
  A traitor to his God, his king, and him,
  And dares him to set forward to the fight.
SECOND HERALD: Here standeth Thomas Mowbray Duke of
  Norfolk,   110
  On pain to be found false and recreant,
  Both to defend himself, and to approve
  Henry of Herford, Lancaster, and Derby

117 *Sound . . . combatants.* In a trial by combat the opponents were on horseback (as Holinshed records in this affair), but it has not been shown that horses were brought on to the Elizabethan stage. How can it be arranged?

118 *thrown . . . down.* The formal signal for stopping the fight. *warder,* truncheon or staff.

120 *chairs.* See note to s.d. l. 25.

122 *While,* until. *return,* inform.
 s.d. *A long flourish* F only. Richard and his councillors may gather round his throne or retreat into the 'discovery space'.

129– *And . . . sleep.* Not in F. As the text stands in Q, 'peace' (l. 132) is
33 'roused up' (l. 134) to 'fright fair peace' (l. 137) and the passage is not clear. Either F attempted to improve the sense, or the lines were marked for deletion in the manuscript copy consulted by F, and the Q compositor failed to observe, or ignored, the deletion marks. Wells suggests that 'it is just as likely that Shakespeare lost control of his metaphors'.

129– *eagle-winged . . . thoughts.* See I. i. 109. Richard again hints at
30 Bolingbroke's intentions.

131 *on you,* you on.

140 *upon . . . life,* i.e. upon penalty of losing your life.

142 *regreet,* greet again.

68

To God, his sovereign, and to him disloyal,
Courageously, and with a free desire,
Attending but the signal to begin.
LORD MARSHAL: Sound trumpets, and set forward combatants.
　　　　　　　　　　　　　　　　　[*A charge sounded*
Stay, the King hath thrown his warder down.
KING RICHARD: Let them lay by their helmets and their spears,
And both return back to their chairs again.　　　　　　120
[*To his Lords*]
Withdraw with us, and let the trumpets sound
While we return these dukes what we decree.
　　　　　　　　　　　　　　　　　　　[*A long flourish*

[*To Bolingbroke and Mowbray*] Draw near,
And list what with our council we have done.
For that our kingdom's earth should not be soiled
With that dear blood which it hath fostered;
And for our eyes do hate the dire aspect
Of civil wounds ploughed up with neighbours' sword;
And for we think the eagle-winged pride
Of sky-aspiring and ambitious thoughts　　　　　　130
With rival-hating envy set on you
To wake our peace, which in our country's cradle
Draws the sweet infant-breath of gentle sleep;
Which so roused up with boisterous untuned drums,
With harsh-resounding trumpets' dreadful bray,
And grating shock of wrathful iron arms,
Might from our quiet confines fright fair peace,
And make us wade even in our kindred's blood;
Therefore we banish you our territories.
You cousin Herford, upon pain of life　　　　　　140
Till twice five summers have enriched our fields,
Shall not regreet our fair dominions,

143   *stranger*, alien, foreign.
       Some see hypocrisy in Richard's intervention, impartiality, and claim to seek peace; others see cowardice, or political expediency.
       Is Richard's sentence—ill-advised, unjust, correct, merciful, unavoidable?

144–7 *This . . . banishment.* In view of the 'sun'–'king' image, is there prophetic irony here? That the sun shines on all alike—the good and the evil, was proverbial. Is the rhyme—emphatic, indicating finality, hypocrisy, or dignity?

148   *doom*, punishment.

150   *sly*, stealthy, imperceptible. *determinate*, put an end to.

151   *dateless limit*, limitless period. *dear*, bitter (dire).

154   *sentence.* Perhaps a bitter reference to 'word' in l. 152.

156   *A . . . maim*, a more valuable recompense, not so severe an injury. Mowbray claims that he deserves a reward—for Gloucester's death, for other services rendered, or merely that he is innocent?

162   *viol.* A stringed instrument, usually the viol de gamba, played on or between the knees with a bow.

163   *cunning*, i.e. that requires skill in playing, or perhaps skilfully made.

165   *touch*, fingering, skill.

167   *portcullised.* The portcullis was a strong grating lowered as part of the gate barring entrance to a fortress.

170   *to . . . nurse*, i.e. to learn to speak as a baby does from its nurse.

172   *speechless.* As a dead man is speechless, Mowbray, unable to speak a foreign tongue, in exile is as dead. Perhaps a bitter glance at 'sentence'.

173   *breathing native breath*, (a) speaking his own language, (b) breathing English air.

But tread the stranger paths of banishment.
BOLINGBROKE: Your will be done. This must my comfort be,
    That sun that warms you here shall shine on me,
    And those his golden beams to you here lent
    Shall point on me, and gild my banishment.
KING RICHARD: Norfolk, for thee remains a heavier doom,
    Which I with some unwillingness pronounce.
    The sly slow hours shall not determinate   150
    The dateless limit of thy dear exile.
    The hopeless word of 'never to return'
    Breathe I against thee, upon pain of life.
MOWBRAY: A heavy sentence, my most sovereign liege,
    And all unlooked for from your highness' mouth.
    A dearer merit, not so deep a maim
    As to be cast forth in the common air,
    Have I deserved at your highness' hands.
    The language I have learnt these forty years,
    My native English, now I must forgo,   160
    And now my tongue's use is to me no more
    Than an unstringed viol or a harp,
    Or like a cunning instrument cased up—
    Or being open, put into his hands
    That knows no touch to tune the harmony.
    Within my mouth you have engaoled my tongue,
    Doubly portcullised with my teeth and lips,
    And dull unfeeling barren ignorance
    Is made my gaoler to attend on me.
    I am too old to fawn upon a nurse,   170
    Too far in years to be a pupil now.
    What is thy sentence then but speechless death,
    Which robs my tongue from breathing native breath?

174   *It . . . be*, it is no use to be. *compassionate*, (a) sorry for yourself, (b) looking for pity.

175   *plaining*, complaining.

       Is Richard—annoyed, abrupt, fearful, callous, indifferent, quick to prevent Mowbray from further speech?

178   *take an oath*. Oath-taking and oath-breaking are important parts of the play's design. An oath was very much more than a promise.

179   *Lay . . . sword*, i.e. on the cross formed by the hilt, blade, and guard.

181   *Our . . . yourselves*, my share in that duty as God's deputy I absolve you from.

188   *advised*, deliberate.

189   *complot*, join in plotting.

193   *far*. Q and F have 'fare', which Dover Wilson interprets, 'Bol. will not bid Mow. fare*well* but only the 'fare' (= condition of life) he would wish as to an enemy'. But to render it, 'I will say thus much to you as an enemy', seems satisfactory.

202   *My . . . life*. An echo of *Rev.*, iii. 5: 'He that overcometh, shall be thus clothed in white array, and I will not blot out his name out of the book of life'.

204-5   *But . . . rue*. Why does Shakespeare remind the audience of the future?

206-7   *Now . . . way*, now I cannot go astray, for I can go anywhere in the world except England.

KING RICHARD: It boots thee not to be compassionate.
  After our sentence plaining comes too late.
MOWBRAY: Then thus I turn me from my country's light,
  To dwell in solemn shades of endless night.
KING RICHARD: Return again, and take an oath with thee.
  Lay on our royal sword your banished hands;
  Swear by the duty that you owe to God—   180
  Our part therein we banish with yourselves—
  To keep the oath that we administer:
  You never shall, so help you truth and God,
  Embrace each other's love in banishment,
  Nor never look upon each other's face,
  Nor never write, regreet, nor reconcile
  This lowering tempest of your home-bred hate,
  Nor never by advised purpose meet
  To plot, contrive, or complot any ill
  'Gainst us, our state, our subjects, or our land.   190
BOLINGBROKE: I swear.
MOWBRAY: And I, to keep all this.
BOLINGBROKE: Norfolk, so far as to mine enemy:
  By this time, had the King permitted us,
  One of our souls had wandered in the air,
  Banished this frail sepulchre of our flesh,
  As now our flesh is banished from this land.
  Confess thy reasons ere thou fly the realm;
  Since thou hast far to go, bear not along
  The clogging burden of a guilty soul.   200
MOWBRAY: No Bolingbroke, if ever I were traitor,
  My name be blotted from the book of life,
  And I from heaven banished as from hence.
  But what thou art, God, thou, and I do know,
  And all too soon, I fear, the King shall rue.
  Farewell, my liege. Now no way can I stray—
  Save back to England all the world's my way.   *[Exit*

208　*glasses . . . eyes*, i.e. mirrors reflecting his feelings.
　　　　Is Richard's action—impulsive, premeditated, cynical, unjust, nepotic, gracious, changeable?

214　*wanton*, luxuriant.
　　　　Is Bolingbroke—shocked, envious, bitter, contemptuous, glad, sorrowful, grateful?

220　*bring . . . about*, complete their cycles.

221　*oil-dried . . . light*. See *1 Henry VI*, II. v. 8–9, where Mortimer dying says, 'These eyes like lamps whose wasting oil is spent, Wax dim'.

222　*extinct with*, extinguished by.

223　*inch . . . done*. The image is frequently used by Shakespeare. See *Macbeth*, V. v. 23.

224　*blindfold death*. Not found elsewhere in Shakespeare. S. Chew (*Pilgrimage of Life*, p. 234) suggests 'struck blind', the original meaning of 'blindfold' (see O.E.D.), but E. Panofsky (*Studies in Iconology*, pp. 111–2) notes that Death was portrayed as having a bandage over the eyes.

227　*sullen*, gloomy.

230　*But . . . pilgrimage*, but not prevent the wrinkles made on me as time journeys on. *his pilgrimage*. See *Lucrece*, l. 960.

231　*current*, i.e. as valid as a current coin. The image is continued in 'buy'.

234　*party-verdict*, one person's share of a joint verdict.

235　*lour*, frown.

236　*Things . . . sour*. Proverbial. See *Lucrece*, l. 699, 'His taste delicious, in digestion souring'. Probably derived from *Rev.*, x. 10, 'it was in my mouth as sweet as honey; and as soon as I had eaten it, my belly was bitter'.

239–　*O . . . destroyed*. Not in F.
42

241　*partial slander*, accusation of partiality.

KING RICHARD: Uncle, even in the glasses of thine eyes
  I see thy grieved heart. Thy sad aspect
  Hath from the number of his banished years   210
  Plucked four away. [*To Bolingbroke*] Six frozen winters spent,
  Return with welcome home from banishment.
BOLINGBROKE: How long a time lies in one little word.
  Four lagging winters and four wanton springs
  End in a word—such is the breath of kings.
JOHN OF GAUNT: I thank my liege that in regard of me
  He shortens four years of my son's exile,
  But little vantage shall I reap thereby;
  For ere the six years that he hath to spend
  Can change their moons, and bring their times about,   220
  My oil-dried lamp and time-bewasted light
  Shall be extinct with age and endless night;
  My inch of taper will be burnt and done,
  And blindfold death not let me see my son.
KING RICHARD: Why uncle, thou hast many years to live.
JOHN OF GAUNT: But not a minute, King, that thou canst give.
  Shorten my days thou canst with sullen sorrow,
  And pluck nights from me, but not lend a morrow.
  Thou canst help time to furrow me with age,
  But stop no wrinkle in his pilgrimage.   230
  Thy word is current with him for my death,
  But dead, thy kingdom cannot buy my breath.
KING RICHARD: Thy son is banished upon good advice
  Whereto thy tongue a party-verdict gave.
  Why at our justice seemest thou then to lour?
JOHN OF GAUNT: Things sweet to taste prove in digestion sour.
  You urged me as a judge, but I had rather
  You would have bid me argue like a father.
  O had it been a stranger, not my child,
  To smooth his fault I should have been more mild.   240
  A partial slander sought I to avoid,

243 *looked when*, expected that.

249– *what . . . show*, as we cannot longer meet (because Bolingbroke is
50   an exile), let me know by letter where you are.
       Presumably Aumerle leaves the stage at this point for he enters
at the beginning of the next scene. Yet he accompanies Bolingbroke 'to the next highway' (I. iv. 4), although he has made a
formal farewell here.

256 *office*, function. *prodigal*, profuse.
257 *To breathe*, in uttering.
258 *grief*, complaint, grievance.
259 *grief*, sorrow. A quibble.

262 *travel*, (a) journeying, (b) travail, labour.

264 *enforced pilgrimage*. A bitter contradiction since a pilgrimage is
essentially voluntary.
265 *sullen*, (a) dull, (b) sad.
266 *foil*, setting to enhance a jewel by contrast. Bolingbroke takes up
'foil' as 'frustration', 'obstacle' to fashion the bitter word-play of
his reply (Mahood, *Shakespeare's Wordplay*, p. 78).
269 *remember*, remind.
270 *jewels*, precious things.

And in the sentence my own life destroyed.
Alas, I looked when some of you should say
I was too strict, to make mine own away.
But you gave leave to my unwilling tongue
Against my will to do myself this wrong.

KING RICHARD: Cousin farewell—and uncle, bid him so.
Six years we banish him, and he shall go.

                [*Flourish. Exit King Richard with his train*

AUMERLE: Cousin farewell, what presence must not know,
From where you do remain let paper show.   250

LORD MARSHAL: My lord, no leave take I, for I will ride
As far as land will let me by your side.

JOHN OF GAUNT: O to what purpose dost thou hoard thy
    words,
That thou returnest no greeting to thy friends?

BOLINGBROKE: I have too few to take my leave of you,
When the tongue's office should be prodigal
To breathe the abundant dolour of the heart.

JOHN OF GAUNT: Thy grief is but thy absence for a time.

BOLINGBROKE: Joy absent, grief is present for that time.   259

JOHN OF GAUNT: What is six winters? They are quickly gone.

BOLINGBROKE: To men in joy, but grief makes one hour ten.

JOHN OF GAUNT: Call it a travel that thou takest for pleasure.

BOLINGBROKE: My heart will sigh when I miscall it so,
Which finds it an enforced pilgrimage.

JOHN OF GAUNT: The sullen passage of thy weary steps
Esteem as foil wherein thou art to set
The precious jewel of thy home return.

BOLINGBROKE: Nay rather, every tedious stride I make
Will but remember me what a deal of world
I wander from the jewels that I love.   270

271–4 *Must . . . grief?* The 'apprentice' image is extended through 'serve', 'apprenticehood', 'freedom', 'journeyman'—with a pun on the last.

275–6 *All . . . havens.* Proverbially a wise man makes every country his own.

276 *havens.* Perhaps punning on 'heavens'.

278 *There . . . necessity.* Proverbial.

279–80 *Think . . . King.* Is this prophetic irony?

280–1 *Woe . . . borne.* Proverbial. See ll. 292–3.

281 *faintly*, faint-heartedly.

282 *purchase*, win.

286 *Look what*, whatever.

289 *the presence strewed*, the royal presence-chamber strewed with rushes.

291 *measure*, stately dance.

292–3 *For . . . light.* Proverbial.

292 *gnarling*, snarling.

294–301 *O . . . worse.* Bolingbroke extends Gaunt's argument in practical terms to the absurd. Does he lack imagination?

296 *cloy*, satisfy, surfeit.

299 *fantastic*, imagined.

302–3 *Fell . . . sore*, i.e. the festering wound made by the biting of sorrow hurts more than the curative wound made by a lancet.

Must I not serve a long apprenticehood
To foreign passages, and in the end,
Having my freedom, boast of nothing else
But that I was a journeyman to grief?
JOHN OF GAUNT: All places that the eye of heaven visits
Are to a wise man ports and happy havens.
Teach thy necessity to reason thus:
There is no virtue like necessity.
Think not the King did banish thee,
But thou the King. Woe doth the heavier sit   280
Where it perceives it is but faintly borne.
Go, say I sent thee forth to purchase honour,
And not the King exiled thee; or suppose
Devouring pestilence hangs in our air,
And thou art flying to a fresher clime.
Look what thy soul holds dear, imagine it
To lie that way thou goest, not whence thou comest.
Suppose the singing birds musicians,
The grass whereon thou treadest the presence strewed,
The flowers fair ladies, and thy steps no more   290
Than a delightful measure or a dance;
For gnarling sorrow hath less power to bite
The man that mocks at it and sets it light.
BOLINGBROKE: O who can hold a fire in his hand
By thinking on the frosty Caucasus?
Or cloy the hungry edge of appetite
By bare imagination of a feast?
Or wallow naked in December snow
By thinking on fantastic summer's heat?
O no, the apprehension of the good   300
Gives but the greater feeling to the worse.
Fell sorrow's tooth doth never rankle more
Than when he bites, but lanceth not the sore.

304   *bring*, accompany.

307   *My . . . yet*. See II. i. 51. *bears*, sustains.

309   *a trueborn Englishman*. Is this national pride or a glance at the rumour that Richard, born at Bordeaux, was the illegitimate son of a French priest. See note to IV. i. 254–6.

    The scene moves from formal phrasing, ritual pageantry, and dignified exchanges between the protagonists to their embittered emotional responses on the level of personal enmity, and the threat to national stability. The implication of Richard in Gloucester's death is not mentioned but the limitations of his authority are exposed. Themes touched on are—blood, love of country, honour, oath-taking. 'Tongue' (speech, words), and 'sorrow' and 'grief' stressed in this scene are words which occur more often in this play than in any other of Shakespeare's plays.

The Court

S.D.   Q has 'Enter the King with Bushie etc., at one dore, and the Lord Aumarle at another'; F has 'Enter King, Aumerle, Greene and Bagot'. Shakespeare apparently intended to introduce the three favourites here, but later decided to have Bushy bring the news of Gaunt's illness.

1   *We did observe*, i.e. Bolingbroke's 'courtship to the common people'. See ll. 23–36.

2   *high*, proud.

4   *highway*. Is Aumerle's quibble—flippant, cynical, scornful, frivolous, contemptuous?

6   *for me*, on my part. *except*, except that.

8   *Awaked . . . rheum*, made our eyes water.

12   *for*, because.

JOHN OF GAUNT: Come, come, my son, I'll bring thee on thy
way.
  Had I thy youth and cause, I would not stay.
BOLINGBROKE: Then England's ground, farewell; sweet soil,
    adieu,
  My mother and my nurse that bears me yet.
  Where'er I wander, boast of this I can,
  Though banished, yet a trueborn Englishman.   [*Exeunt*

SCENE FOUR

Enter the KING *with* BAGOT *and* GREEN *at one door,*
and the LORD AUMERLE *at another*

KING RICHARD: We did observe. Cousin Aumerle,
  How far brought you high Herford on his way?
AUMERLE: I brought high Herford, if you call him so,
  But to the next highway, and there I left him.
KING RICHARD: And say, what store of parting tears were shed?
AUMERLE: Faith none for me, except the north-east wind,
  Which then blew bitterly against our faces,
  Awaked the sleeping rheum, and so by chance
  Did grace our hollow parting with a tear.
KING RICHARD: What said our cousin when you parted with
    him?   10
AUMERLE: 'Farewell'—
  And for my heart disdained that my tongue

13   *that*, i.e. 'for . . . word'.

13–15 *craft . . . grave*, skill to pretend to be overcome by so great a grief that it swallowed up all my words as in a grave.

20   *He . . . cousin.* Richard, Bolingbroke, and **A**umerle were cousins. Is this a mild rebuke?

20–2 *but . . . friends.* Either a hint that Bolingbroke may not be recalled from banishment to see his cousins when the six years have passed, or that he will return as an enemy.

23   *Ourself and Bushy* Q. By printing a comma after 'friends', F identifies them as 'Ourself and Bushy'. F continues 'here Bagot and Green', which may retain traces of Shakespeare's original intention. See note to S.D. above.

28   *craftsmen, craft.* A sneering quibble.

29   *underbearing*, enduring.

30   *banish . . . him*, take away with him into banishment their affections which should be given to me, their king.

33   *tribute . . . knee*, acknowledgement of a curtsy.

35   *As . . . his*, as if my England were to return to him as of right after my death.

36   *subjects' . . . hope*, the object of my subjects' hopes after me.
       This speech contains indignation, sarcasm, and irony.

39   *Expedient manage*, speedy arrangements.

43–4 *for . . . light.* Richard's large and extravagant court was notorious.

43   *for*, because.

Should so profane the word, that taught me craft
To counterfeit oppression of such grief
That words seemed buried in my sorrow's grave.
Marry would the word 'farewell' have lengthened hours
And added years to his short banishment,
He should have had a volume of farewells;
But since it would not, he had none of me.

KING RICHARD: He is our cousin, cousin, but 'tis doubt,   20
When time shall call him home from banishment,
Whether our kinsmen come to see his friends.
Ourself and Bushy
Observed his courtship to the common people,
How he did seem to dive into their hearts
With humble and familiar courtesy;
What reverence he did throw away on slaves,
Wooing poor craftsmen with the craft of smiles
And patient underbearing of his fortune,
As 'twere to banish their affects with him.   30
Off goes his bonnet to an oyster-wench;
A brace of draymen bid God speed him well,
And had the tribute of his supple knee,
With 'Thanks, my countrymen, my loving friends',
As were our England in reversion his,
And he our subjects' next degree in hope.

GREEN: Well, he is gone; and with him go these thoughts.
Now for the rebels which stand out in Ireland,
Expedient manage must be made my liege,
Ere further leisure yield them further means   40
For their advantage, and your highness' loss.

KING RICHARD: We will ourself in person to this war;
And, for our coffers with too great a court
And liberal largess are grown somewhat light,

45   *to . . . realm.* Richard granted to his favourites what profit they could make from the royal rents, taxes, customs' dues, in return for the immediate payments of a fixed sum.

48   *substitutes*, deputies, agents.

48–50   *blank . . . gold.* Blank charters were documents in which the signer promised to pay a sum of money. Wealthy persons were forced to sign these, and the King's agents later filled in the amount to be paid.

50   *subscribe them for,* put them down for.

While Richard admits his costly court, his devices are to finance the expedition to Ireland and not to enhance his extravagances. Does he show tenderness for the poor or mere practicality in fleecing the wealthy?

59–60   *Now . . . immediately.* Is Richard—callous, malicious, blasphemous, cynical, astute?

61   *lining*, contents. Perhaps a quibble on coat-linings.

This scene is markedly different in style from the ceremonious and emotional expressions of I. iii. The almost colloquial nature of the verse and the sparseness of imagery accompanies the revelation of Richard's jealousy of Bolingbroke and his naïve opportunism. There is no indication that he is being led astray by flatterers.

We are enforced to farm our royal realm,
The revenue whereof shall furnish us
For our affairs in hand. If that come short,
Our substitutes at home shall have blank charters,
Whereto, when they shall know what men are rich,
They shall subscribe them for large sums of gold,   50
And send them after to supply our wants;
For we will make Ireland presently.

Enter BUSHY

Bushy, what news?
BUSHY: Old John of Gaunt is grievous sick my lord,
     Suddenly taken, and hath sent post-haste
     To entreat your majesty to visit him.
KING RICHARD: Where lies he?
BUSHY: At Ely House.
KING RICHARD: Now put it, God, in the physician's mind
     To help him to his grave immediately.   60
     The lining of his coffers shall make coats
     To deck our soldiers for these Irish wars.
     Come gentlemen, let's all go visit him.
     Pray God we may make haste and come too late.
ALL: Amen.   [*Exeunt*

Ely House

S.D. Gaunt is probably carried in on a chair as is Lear (*King Lear*, IV. vii. 20, F).

2 *unstaid youth*, uncontrolled youth. Writers contemporary with Richard, followed by later chroniclers, stress Richard's youthfulness, although at the time the play begins he was thirty-one years old.

3 *breath*, (a) speech, (b) breath. See l. 30.

5–8 *the . . . pain*. It was a common belief that dying men's words were truthful and prophetically inspired. See *Merchant of Venice*, I. ii. 24–5, 'holy men at their death have good inspirations'.

7–16 *Where . . . ear*. The rhyme pattern serves to mark the 'sentences', wise sayings, or as some think the 'lyrical exaltation' that 'characterizes Gaunt's visionary mood'.

11 *glose*, flatter.

12 *close*, cadence, closing phrase of a musical movement.

13 *As . . . last*. The inversion, antimetabole, concentrates the thought. *sweetest last*, sweetest longest, or, because it comes last.

16 *My . . . tale*, my solemn dying words.

18 *As . . . fond*, i.e. even wise men are fond of praise, or, even wise men are made foolish by praise. Q has 'found'. The emendation 'th'unwise are fond' is a tempting one.

19 *Lascivious metres*, sensuous verses. *venom*, poisonous, corrupting.

ACT TWO

SCENE ONE

Enter JOHN OF GAUNT *sick, with the* DUKE OF YORK *and others*

JOHN OF GAUNT: Will the King come, that I may breathe
  my last
  In wholesome counsel to his unstaid youth?
YORK: Vex not yourself, nor strive not with your breath,
  For all in vain comes counsel to his ear.
JOHN OF GAUNT: O but they say the tongues of dying men
  Enforce attention like deep harmony.
  Where words are scarce they are seldom spent in vain,
  For they breathe truth that breathe their words in pain.
  He that no more must say is listened more
    Than they whom youth and ease have taught to glose;   10
  More are men's ends marked than their lives before.
    The setting sun, and music at the close,
  As the last taste of sweets, is sweetest last,
  Writ in remembrance more than things long past.
  Though Richard my life's counsel would not hear,
  My death's sad tale may yet undeaf his ear.
YORK: No, it is stopped with other, flattering sounds,
  As praises, of whose taste the wise are fond,
  Lascivious metres, to whose venom sound
  The open ear of youth doth always listen,   20

21–3   *Report . . . imitation.* Richard's court was notorious for its extravagant foreign style clothes (Holinshed), but Shakespeare here may have in mind current attacks on imported fashions. See *Merchant of Venice*, I. ii. 62–5.

22   *still,* always. *tardy-apish,* sluggishly imitative.

25   *there's . . . vile,* it's no matter how worthless.

26   *buzzed,* murmured.

28   *will . . . regard,* desire rebels against the views of reason. The opposition of 'erected wit' and 'infected will' was the accepted Elizabethan belief about behaviour, character, and motive.

30   *'Tis . . . lose,* you are short of breath, don't waste words.

31–2   *Methinks . . . foretell.* Gaunt takes up York's play upon 'breath' with 'new-inspired' and quibbles paradoxically with 'expiring'.

33–4   *His . . . themselves.* Proverbial. See *1 Henry IV*, III. ii. 60–2, 'The skipping king, (Richard II) he ambled up and down With shallow jesters and rash bavin wits, Soon kindled and soon burnt.'

33   *rash,* quick. *blaze,* short burst of flame. *riot,* uncontrolled behaviour.

34–9   *For . . . itself.* These 'sentences' on the theme that violence is self-destructive form a prophetic prelude to Gaunt's visionary 'praise' of England.

36   *betimes,* (a) soon, (b) early.

38–9   *Light . . . itself,* idle vanity, that never-satisfied glutton, eating up that which feeds it, soon devours itself. See *Coriolanus*, I. i. 191–2; *Troilus and Cressida*, I. iii. 121–4.

40–58   *This . . . world.* Shakespeare expresses in memorable words many current patriotic views, some of which also occur in medieval writings.

41   *earth of majesty,* land the rightful home of kings. *seat of Mars,* dwelling-place of Mars, the god of war.

42   *other,* second. *demi-paradise,* (a) little paradise, (b) as if it were a paradise.

44   *infection,* corruption. See ll. 21–3 and note.

45   *happy breed,* fortunate race. *this little world,* i.e. this little world in itself. The idea of England as a world in itself remote from the rest is found in classical authors as well as in Shakespeare's fellow writers. See *Cymbeline*, III. i. 12–13.

49   *envy,* hostility.

Report of fashions in proud Italy,
Whose manners still our tardy-apish nation
Limps after in base imitation.
Where doth the world thrust forth a vanity—
So it be new, there's no respect how vile—
That is not quickly buzzed into his ears?
Then all too late comes counsel to be heard,
Where will doth mutiny with wit's regard.
Direct not him whose way himself will choose;
'Tis breath thou lackest, and that breath wilt thou lose.   30
JOHN OF GAUNT: Methinks I am a prophet new-inspired,
    And thus expiring do foretell of him,
    His rash fierce blaze of riot cannot last,
    For violent fires soon burn out themselves.
    Small showers last long, but sudden storms are short.
    He tires betimes that spurs too fast betimes.
    With eager feeding food doth choke the feeder.
    Light vanity, insatiate cormorant,
    Consuming means, soon preys upon itself.
    This royal throne of kings, this sceptred isle,   40
    This earth of majesty, this seat of Mars,
    This other Eden, demi-paradise,
    This fortress built by nature for herself
    Against infection and the hand of war,
    This happy breed of men, this little world,
    This precious stone set in the silver sea,
    Which serves it in the office of a wall,
    Or as a moat defensive to a house,
    Against the envy of less happier lands;
    This blessed plot, this earth, this realm, this England,   50

51   *teeming*, fertile.

54   *Christian service*, i.e. crusades.

55   *stubborn Jewry*, the lands of the Jews. They were stubborn in the
O.T. by disobeying God, and in the N.T. by rejecting Christ.

56   *ransom.* See *Matt.*, xx. 28, 'the son of man came . . . to give his
life a ransom for many'.

60   *tenement*, estate held by a tenant. *pelting*, paltry.

61   *bound in with*, (a) surrounded by, (b) constrained by.

64   *With . . . bonds.* A reference to the forced loans and blank charters.
See I. iv. 48.

65–6   *That . . . itself.* Dover Wilson suggests that the passage in *King
John*, V. vii. 112–14, 'This England never did, nor never shall, Lie
at the proud foot of a conqueror, But when it first did help to
wound itself' reads like a first draft of these lines. This patriotic
sentiment was very common.

70   *raged* Q; F 'ragde', Dover Wilson reads 'ragged'=unbroken,
unruly, as in the proverb, 'A ragged colt may prove a good horse'.
Arden emends to 'reined'. Editors find difficulty in accepting the
line as it stands, but Shakespeare elsewhere repeats the word 'rage'
in the same line: *Lucrece*, l. 1419, 'And in their rage such signs of
rage they bear'; *Troilus and Cressida*, I. iii. 49–54, 'but when the
splitting wind Makes flexible the knees of knotted oaks, And
flies fled under shade, why then the thing of courage As roused
with rage, with rage doth sympathize, And with an accent tuned
in self same key Retorts to chiding fortune'.

York throughout this scene acts as conciliator and temporizer,
a mood he extends later in II. iii.

73   *composition*, condition of mind and body.

This nurse, this teeming womb of royal kings,
Feared by their breed, and famous by their birth,
Renowned for their deeds as far from home,
For Christian service and true chivalry,
As is the sepulchre in stubborn Jewry
Of the world's ransom, blessed Mary's son.
This land of such dear souls, this dear dear land,
Dear for her reputation through the world,
Is now leased out—I die pronouncing it—
Like to a tenement or pelting farm. 60
England, bound in with the triumphant sea,
Whose rocky shore beats back the envious siege
Of watery Neptune, is now bound in with shame,
With inky blots and rotten parchment bonds.
That England that was wont to conquer others,
Hath made a shameful conquest of itself.
Ah would the scandal vanish with my life,
How happy then were my ensuing death!

Enter KING, QUEEN, AUMERLE, BUSHY, GREEN, BAGOT,
ROSS, *and* WILLOUGHBY

YORK: The King is come; deal mildly with his youth,
For young hot colts being raged do rage the more. 70
QUEEN ISABEL: How fares our noble uncle Lancaster?
KING RICHARD: What comfort, man? How is't with aged
Gaunt?
JOHN OF GAUNT: O how that name befits my composition!
Old Gaunt indeed, and gaunt in being old.

75   *grief . . . fast*. Grief was supposed to cause wasting away, and sometimes fasting was observed to express grief.

77   *sleeping*, sluggish. *watched*, (a) kept guard at night, (b) lain awake in anxiety.

80   *Is . . . fast*, I have to do without.

83   *inherits . . . bones*, receives only bones as a bequest.

84   *nicely*, (a) triflingly, (b) ingeniously.

85   *misery . . . itself*, wretchedness, not sickness, finds fun in jeering at itself.

86   *kill . . . me*, i.e. by banishing my son.
      The single verse line exchanges are a device known as stichomythia.

94   *Ill . . . ill*, i.e. because I am ill my sight is impaired and I can only see you dimly, and I see only an evil (ill) king. The inversion of phrases is an anaphora that emphasizes the notion.

100   *crown*, (a) actual crown, (b) the royal court.

101   *compass*, circle.

102   *verge*, (a) boundary, (b) the land within a twelve-mile radius from the king's court, (c) metal rim of a diadem.

103   *waste*, (a) extravagance, (b) damage done to property by a tenant.

104   *grandsire*, Edward III.

105   *son's son*, Richard. *sons*, Gloucester and Gaunt.

Within me grief hath kept a tedious fast,
And who abstains from meat that is not gaunt?
For sleeping England long time have I watched,
Watching breeds leanness, leanness is all gaunt.
The pleasure that some fathers feed upon
Is my strict fast—I mean my children's looks,   80
And therein fasting hast thou made me gaunt.
Gaunt am I for the grave, gaunt as a grave,
Whose hollow womb inherits naught but bones.

KING RICHARD: Can sick men play so nicely with their names?

JOHN OF GAUNT: No, misery makes sport to mock itself.
  Since thou dost seek to kill my name in me,
  I mock my name, great King, to flatter thee.

KING RICHARD: Should dying men flatter with those that live?

JOHN OF GAUNT: No, no, men living flatter those that die.

KING RICHARD: Thou now a-dying sayst thou flatterest me. 90

JOHN OF GAUNT: O no, thou diest, though I the sicker be.

KING RICHARD: I am in health, I breathe, and see thee ill.

JOHN OF GAUNT: Now he that made me knows I see thee ill,
  Ill in myself to see, and in thee, seeing ill.
  Thy death-bed is no lesser than thy land,
  Wherein thou liest in reputation sick;
  And thou, too careless patient as thou art,
  Committest thy anointed body to the cure
  Of those physicians that first wounded thee.
  A thousand flatterers sit within thy crown,   100
  Whose compass is no bigger than thy head,
  And yet, encaged in so small a verge,
  The waste is no whit lesser than thy land.
  O had thy grandsire with a prophet's eye
  Seen how his son's son should destroy his sons,
  From forth thy reach he would have laid thy shame,

107–8 *Deposing . . . thyself.* An anaphora.
107, *possessed*, i.e. crowned. *possessed*, i.e. possessed by an evil spirit.
108

111 *But . . . land*, but as this country you rule is your whole world.

114 *Thy . . . law*, your legal standing is now subject to the law.
    Richard as a landlord is under the law, as a king he should be above the law.
115 *And . . . fool.* Richard turns Gaunt's words against him. *lean-witted*, i.e. gaunt-witted (Dover Wilson).
116 *ague's privilege*, i.e. the privilege allowed you because you are ill. *ague's*, fever's. The ague was a fever with alternating fits of heat and cold, hence 'frozen' (l. 117).
120 *seat's*, throne's.
121 *son*, i.e. Richard's father, the Black Prince.
122 *roundly*, (a) volubly, (b) bluntly.

126 *pelican.* According to Christian legend the pelican, which was believed to feed its young with blood from its own breast, was a symbol of Christ's redemption of the world. A young pelican was an emblem of ingratitude.
129 *whom fair befall*, may blessing be his.
130 *precedent*, example.
131 *That . . . not*, that no respect keeps you from.

133 *unkindness*, unnaturalness. *crooked age.* The idea was common but it may have suggested the harvesting image of time's bent scythe in the next line.
136 *thy tormentors be*, i.e. sting your conscience.
    Gaunt's accusations match his earlier speeches. Richard's lack of care for England contrasts with Gaunt's passionate care. Richard, unlike his ancestors, is subject to flattery and has become not a king but a landlord of this 'little world'. Finally, he despises the royal breed and murders his kin.

Deposing thee before thou wert possessed,
Which art possessed now to depose thyself.
Why cousin, wert thou regent of the world,
It were a shame to let this land by lease.   110
But for thy world enjoying but this land,
Is it not more than shame to shame it so?
Landlord of England art thou now, not king;
Thy state of law is bondslave to the law,
And thou—

KING RICHARD: —A lunatic lean-witted fool,
Presuming on an ague's privilege,
Darest with thy frozen admonition
Make pale our cheek, chasing the royal blood
With fury from his native residence.
Now by my seat's right royal majesty,   120
Wert thou not brother to great Edward's son,
This tongue that runs so roundly in thy head
Should run thy head from thy unreverent shoulders.

JOHN OF GAUNT: O, spare me not, my brother Edward's son,
For that I was his father Edward's son.
That blood already, like the pelican,
Hast thou tapped out and drunkenly caroused.
My brother Gloucester, plain well-meaning soul,
Whom fair befall in heaven 'mongst happy souls,
May be a precedent and witness good   130
That thou respectest not spilling Edward's blood.
Join with the present sickness that I have,
And thy unkindness be like crooked age,
To crop at once a too long withered flower.
Live in thy shame, but die not shame with thee.
These words hereafter thy tormentors be.
Convey me to my bed, then to my grave.
Love they to live that love and honour have.

[Exit with attendants

139   *sullens*, sulks.

145–6 *Right . . . is*. Is Richard—enraged, cynical, callous, indifferent, flippant, contemptuous?

151   *bankrupt*. This carries on the thought in 'spent' (l. 150) and is extended in 'poor' (l. 152).

152   *death*, being dead. *mortal*, (a) human, (b) deadly.

153   *The . . . he*. Proverbial. See *Merchant of Venice*, IV. 1. 115–16.

154   *our . . . be*, our journey through life must go on.

156   *rug-headed kerns*, shaggy-headed Irish foot soldiers.

157   *where . . . else*. A reference to Ireland's freedom from snakes, which, according to legend, were banished by St Patrick.

159   *ask some charge*, demand great expense.

164   *tender*, solicitous, scrupulous. *suffer*, tolerate.

166   *Gaunt's rebukes*, i.e. rebukes directed at Gaunt. *England's private wrongs*, wrongs suffered by private persons in England.

KING RICHARD: And let them die that age and sullens have,
  For both hast thou, and both become the grave.   140
YORK: I do beseech your majesty, impute his words
  To wayward sickliness and age in him.
  He loves you, on my life, and holds you dear
  As Harry Duke of Herford, were he here.
KING RICHARD: Right, you say true; as Herford's love, so his;
  As theirs, so mine; and all be as it is.

Enter NORTHUMBERLAND

NORTHUMBERLAND: My liege, old Gaunt commends him to
  your majesty.
KING RICHARD: What says he?
NORTHUMBERLAND: Nay nothing, all is said.
  His tongue is now a stringless instrument,
  Words, life, and all, old Lancaster hath spent.   150
YORK: Be York the next that must be bankrupt so.
  Though death be poor, it ends a mortal woe.
KING RICHARD: The ripest fruit first falls, and so doth he;
  His time is spent, our pilgrimage must be.
  So much for that. Now for our Irish wars.
  We must supplant those rough rug-headed kerns
  Which live like venom where no venom else
  But only they have privilege to live.
  And for these great affairs do ask some charge,
  Towards our assistance we do seize to us   160
  The plate, coin, revenues, and moveables
  Whereof our uncle Gaunt did stand possessed.
YORK: How long shall I be patient? Ah, how long
  Shall tender duty make me suffer wrong?
  Not Gloucester's death, nor Herford's banishment,
  Nor Gaunt's rebukes, nor England's private wrongs,

167–8 *Nor . . . marriage.* According to Holinshed Bolingbroke in exile
was entertained at the French Court. Arrangements for him to
marry the daughter of the Duke of Berri, cousin of the French
king were thwarted by Richard who alleged 'heinous offences
against him'.

168 *nor his.* This is the reading of the Petworth quarto. The reading
'my' for 'his' in other quartos, the Folio, and later editions leaves
the reference obscure. (See *Shakespeare Survey* 10, p. 151; 11,
p. 152.)

170 *bend . . . face*, made me frown upon my king.

177 *Accomplished . . . hours*, when he was your age.

182–3 *no . . . kin.* Inverted phrasing—anaphora.

185 *between.* York breaks off overcome with grief.

186 *Why . . . matter?* Is Richard—puzzled, callous, mocking, genuinely
solicitous? What has he been doing?

190 *royalties*, rights granted to a subject by the king.

192 *true*, i.e. Bolingbroke had loyally gone into exile.

195 *Take . . . time*, if you take Bolingbroke's rights away it is as if you
take away from time itself.

197 *ensue*, follow.

Nor the prevention of poor Bolingbroke
About his marriage, nor his own disgrace,
Have ever made me sour my patient cheek,
Or bend one wrinkle on my sovereign's face.   170
I am the last of noble Edward's sons,
Of whom thy father, Prince of Wales, was first.
In war was never lion raged more fierce,
In peace was never gentle lamb more mild,
Than was that young and princely gentleman.
His face thou hast, for even so looked he
Accomplished with the number of thy hours;
But when he frowned it was against the French,
And not against his friends. His noble hand
Did win what he did spend, and spent not that   180
Which his triumphant father's hand had won.
His hands were guilty of no kindred blood,
But bloody with the enemies of his kin.
O Richard! York is too far gone with grief,
Or else he never would compare between—
KING RICHARD: Why uncle, what's the matter?
YORK: O my liege,
Pardon me if you please; if not, I pleased
Not to be pardoned, am content withal.
Seek you to seize and gripe into your hands
The royalties and rights of banished Herford?   190
Is not Gaunt dead? And doth not Herford live?
Was not Gaunt just? And is not Harry true?
Did not the one deserve to have an heir?
Is not his heir a well-deserving son?
Take Herford's rights away, and take from time
His charters and his customary rights;
Let not tomorrow then ensue today.

198–9 *Be . . . succession?* York draws an ominous parallel between Bolingbroke's deprivation of rights and the suppositious loss of Richard's rights, both derived from custom and succession.

201 *wrongfully . . . rights.* A quibble.

202–4 *Call . . . livery,* revoke the letters-patent which you granted him to enable him through attorneys to submit a claim for his inheritance.

The letters-patent would have allowed Bolingbroke to institute proceedings to obtain his father's lands which under feudal law would revert to the sovereign until it had been proved that the heir was of age. When the heir received the lands, he was required to make an act of homage to the king.

204 *livery,* delivery of lands or property. *deny . . . homage.* By revoking the letters-patent Richard had made it impossible for the exiled Bolingbroke to claim his inheritance and to pay homage in person.

207–8 *And . . . think.* York's conciliatory and compromising attitude gives way to hinting at treason.

209– *Think . . . good.* The rhymes mark Richard's decisive view, and
14 York's underline them and close the episode.

213– *But . . . good.* Proverbial. See II. iii. 144; *Rom.,* iii. 8.
14

214 *events,* outcomes, results.

215 *Earl of Wiltshire,* William le Scrope, the Treasurer.

216 *Ely House,* i.e. here.

217 *see,* see to.

218 *trow,* think.

220–1 *York . . . well.* A surprising appointment in view of York's protests, but York in Holinshed is a mild and gentle man. Wells notes that this surprising appreciation of York is caused at least partly by Shakespeare's telescoping of events. In Holinshed some time passes between Gaunt's death and Richard's decision to go to Ireland.

228 *great,* swollen with strong feelings.

229 *Ere . . . tongue,* before it can be relieved by speaking freely.

Be not thyself; for how art thou a king
But by fair sequence and succession?
Now afore God—God forbid I say true—   200
If you do wrongfully seize Herford's rights,
Call in the letters patents that he hath
By his attorneys-general to sue
His livery, and deny his offered homage,
You pluck a thousand dangers on your head,
You lose a thousand well-disposed hearts,
And prick my tender patience to those thoughts
Which honour and allegiance cannot think.

KING RICHARD: Think what you will, we seize into our hands
His plate, his goods, his money, and his lands.   210

YORK: I'll not be by the while. My liege farewell.
What will ensue hereof there's none can tell;
But by bad courses may be understood
That their events can never fall out good.   [*Exit*

KING RICHARD: Go Bushy to the Earl of Wiltshire straight,
Bid him repair to us to Ely House
To see this business. Tomorrow next
We will for Ireland, and 'tis time I trow.
And we create in absence of ourself
Our uncle York Lord Governor of England;   220
For he is just and always loved us well.
Come on, our Queen, tomorrow must we part.
Be merry, for our time of stay is short.

[*Flourish. Exeunt King and Queen, Bushy, Bagot, Green.
Northumberland, Willoughby, and Ross remain*

NORTHUMBERLAND: Well lords, the Duke of Lancaster is dead.

ROSS: And living too, for now his son is duke.

WILLOUGHBY: Barely in title, not in revenues.

NORTHUMBERLAND: Richly in both, if justice had her right.

ROSS: My heart is great, but it must break with silence,
Ere't be disburdened with a liberal tongue.

231   *That . . . harm*, who repeats your words to betray you.
232   *Tends . . . to*, does what you would say favour.

239   *moe*, more.

241–2 *The . . . flatterers*. What evidence is there of this?

246   *pilled*, plundered.

250   *blanks*, blank charters which a man was compelled to sign; the amount of money he had to pay was later filled in by the tax agent. *benevolences*, forced loans demanded by the king but described as gifts. *wot*, know.
252–3 *for . . . compromise*. Possibly the surrender of Brest to the Duke of Brittany, 1397, which instigated the quarrel between Richard and the Duke of Gloucester.

256   *in farm*. See note to I. iv. 45.
257   *broken*, ruined financially.

NORTHUMBERLAND: Nay speak thy mind, and let him ne'er
   speak more   230
  That speaks thy words again to do thee harm.
WILLOUGHBY: Tends that thou wouldst speak to the Duke of
   Herford?
  If it be so, out with it boldly, man.
  Quick is mine ear to hear of good towards him.
ROSS: No good at all that I can do for him,
  Unless you call it good to pity him,
  Bereft, and gelded of his patrimony.
NORTHUMBERLAND: Now afore God 'tis shame such wrongs
   are borne
  In him, a royal prince, and many moe
  Of noble blood in this declining land.   240
  The King is not himself, but basely led
  By flatterers; and what they will inform,
  Merely in hate, 'gainst any of us all,
  That will the King severely prosecute
  'Gainst us, our lives, our children, and our heirs.
ROSS: The commons hath he pilled with grievous taxes,
  And quite lost their hearts. The nobles hath he fined
  For ancient quarrels, and quite lost their hearts.
WILLOUGHBY: And daily new exactions are devised,
  As blanks, benevolences, and I wot not what.   250
  But what a God's name doth become of this?
NORTHUMBERLAND: Wars hath not wasted it, for warred he
   hath not,
  But basely yielded upon compromise
  That which his noble ancestors achieved with blows.
  More hath he spent in peace than they in wars.
ROSS: The Earl of Wiltshire hath the realm in farm.
WILLOUGHBY: The King's grown bankrupt like a broken man.
NORTHUMBERLAND: Reproach and dissolution hangeth over
   him.

266   *strike*, (a) lower sails, (b) rebel. *securely*, complacently secure, over-
confident.

268   *unavoided*, unavoidable.

269   *For suffering so*, for so putting up with.

270   *eyes*, eye-sockets.

275   *are but thyself*, are one with you.

278   *Brittaine*, Brittany. *intelligence*, information.

280   *The . . . Arundel*. This line, not in Q or F, was added by Malone
in agreement with the account in Holinshed, for Cobham did not
break from the Duke of Exeter. Arundel was executed in 1397,
and his brother the Archbishop of Canterbury was banished.
Wells makes the interesting suggestion that a line referring to
Arundel was censored because the Earl of Arundel died in prison
convicted of treason in 1595, and Elizabeth attempted to prevent
his son succeeding to the title and inheritance.

281   *broke*, escaped.

286   *tall*, fine.

287   *expedience*, speed.

289   *stay*, wait for.

ROSS: He hath not money for these Irish wars,
  His burdenous taxations notwithstanding,   260
  But by the robbing of the banished Duke.
NORTHUMBERLAND: His noble kinsman—most degenerate
    King.
  But lords, we hear this fearful tempest sing,
  Yet seek no shelter to avoid the storm.
  We see the wind sit sore upon our sails,
  And yet we strike not, but securely perish.
ROSS: We see the very wrack that we must suffer,
  And unavoided is the danger now,
  For suffering so the causes of our wrack.
NORTHUMBERLAND: Not so; even through the hollow eyes
    of death   270
  I spy life peering; but I dare not say
  How near the tidings of our comfort is.
WILLOUGHBY: Nay let us share thy thoughts as thou dost ours.
ROSS: Be confident to speak Northumberland.
  We three are but thyself, and speaking so
  Thy words are but as thoughts; therefore be bold.
NORTHUMBERLAND: Then thus: I have from Le Port Blanc,
  A bay in Brittaine, received intelligence
  That Harry Duke of Herford, Rainold Lord Cobham,
  The son of Richard Earl of Arundel   280
  That late broke from the Duke of Exeter,
  His brother, Archbishop late of Canterbury,
  Sir Thomas Erpingham, Sir John Ramston,
  Sir John Norbery, Sir Robert Waterton, and Francis Coint;
  All these well-furnished by the Duke of Brittaine
  With eight tall ships, three thousand men of war,
  Are making hither with all due expedience,
  And shortly mean to touch our northern shore.
  Perhaps they had ere this, but that they stay
  The first departing of the King for Ireland.   290

292   *Imp*, graft new feathers into the wing of a falcon to improve its flight.

293   *broking pawn*, i.e. those who have lent money to the King and who 'farm' the land.

294   *gilt*, (a) gold, (b) shame (guilt).

296   *post*, haste. *Ravenspurgh*. A seaport, now washed away, near Spurn Head.

297   *you faint*, you are faint-hearted.

300   *Hold . . . horse*, if my horse lasts out.

      I. iv and II. i present Richard unfavourably alongside Gaunt's passionate love for England and York's mood of conciliation and regret. They see him as a hot young colt, subject to flatterers, destroyer of his own family, landlord not king of England. He displays insensitivity, failure to understand his uncles' feelings, incapacity to foresee the results of his actions. With blasphemous cynicism he wishes for Gaunt's speedy death, and with what proves to be a fatal act seizes Gaunt's possessions thereby breaking both law and custom and driving the lords in self-defence to join with Bolingbroke.

Windsor Castle

1   *your majesty*. The Queen, Isabel, is presented as an adult. She was in fact at this time eleven years old, having been married to Richard as his second wife when she was eight.

3   *life-harming heaviness*. Grief was supposed to induce melancholy, which, 'being cold and dry, dryeth the whole body, and maketh it wither away, for cold extinguisheth heat, and dryness moisture, which two qualities principally concern life' (Wright, *Passions of the Mind*, pp. 61–2). See *Ecclus.*, xxx. 23, 'as for sorrow and heaviness, drive it far from thee; for heaviness hath slain many a man'.

7–9   *Why . . . Richard*. See *Romeo and Juliet*, II. ii. 184, 'Parting is such sweet sorrow'.

7   *welcome . . . grief*. See *Pericles*, I. ii. 3.

10–11   *Some . . . me*. See ll. 62–6 for continuation of the image.

If then we shall shake off our slavish yoke,
Imp out our drooping country's broken wing,
Redeem from broking pawn the blemished crown,
Wipe off the dust that hides our sceptre's gilt,
And make high majesty look like itself,
Away with me in post to Ravenspurgh.
But if you faint, as fearing to do so,
Stay, and be secret, and myself will go.
ROSS: To horse, to horse, urge doubts to them that fear.
WILLOUGHBY: Hold out my horse, and I will first be there.

[*Exeunt* 300

SCENE TWO

Enter the QUEEN, BUSHY, *and* BAGOT

BUSHY: Madam, your majesty is too much sad.
You promised, when you parted with the King,
To lay aside life-harming heaviness,
And entertain a cheerful disposition.
QUEEN ISABEL: To please the King I did; to please myself
I cannot do it. Yet I know no cause
Why I should welcome such a guest as grief,
Save bidding farewell to so sweet a guest
As my sweet Richard. Yet again methinks
Some unborn sorrow ripe in fortune's womb   10
Is coming towards me, and my inward soul

14–24   *Each . . . not*, for every real cause of grief there are twenty that appear real but are not. Tears of sorrow blurring the sight split up one whole object into many, just like perspective pictures, which looked at directly show only distorted images, but viewed indirectly reveal distinct forms. So you, regarding from a wrong point of view ('awry') your husband's departure, see more forms that cause grief than he himself causes, but these looked on rightly are only illusory nothings.

17   *Divides . . . objects*. Perspective multiplying glasses were cut with a number of facets each of which gave a distinct image.

18–20   *which . . . form*. Perspective paintings were so contrived that the picture varied according to the position of the spectator, or could not be seen properly except from an unusual position. (See *Shakespeare's England*, II, p. 10.)

31   *though . . . think*, though when I think I think of nothing.

33   *conceit*, fancy.

34   *nothing less*, anything but.

34–8   *Conceit . . . possess*, sad imagining is always fathered by grief. My grief is not so derived for nothing has begotten my very real grief, or something else has the reality of the nothingness that afflicts me, and I possess it only as something held in trust that will revert to me.

34, 35, 36   *Conceit* (conception), *forefather*, *begot*. The image of begetting is repeated here (see ll. 10, 62–6). 'Conceit' can also infer a morbid state of mind.

38   *reversion*, legal passing on. Perhaps a glance at the antimetabole, or turning back on itself, of the previous sentence, 'nothing'–'something'; 'something'–'nothing'. The reversion notion is linked with 'birth' and namelessness in *Troilus and Cressida*, III. ii. 99–102.

With nothing trembles. At something it grieves
More than with parting from my lord the King.
BUSHY: Each substance of a grief hath twenty shadows,
    Which shows like grief itself, but is not so.
    For sorrow's eye, glazed with blinding tears,
    Divides one thing entire to many objects,
    Like perspectives which, rightly gazed upon,
    Show nothing but confusion; eyed awry,
    Distinguish form. So your sweet majesty,   20
    Looking awry upon your lord's departure,
    Find shapes of grief more than himself to wail,
    Which looked on as it is, is naught but shadows
    Of what it is not. Then, thrice-gracious Queen,
    More than your lord's departure weep not, more is not seen;
    Or if it be, 'tis with false sorrow's eye,
    Which for things true weeps things imaginary.
QUEEN ISABEL: It may be so; but yet my inward soul
    Persuades me it is otherwise. Howe'er it be,
    I cannot but be sad; so heavy-sad   30
    As, though on thinking on no thought I think,
    Makes me with heavy nothing faint and shrink.
BUSHY: 'Tis nothing but conceit, my gracious lady.
QUEEN ISABEL: 'Tis nothing less. Conceit is still derived
    From some forefather grief. Mine is not so,
    For nothing hath begot my something grief,
    Or something hath the nothing that I grieve—
    'Tis in reversion that I do possess—
    But what it is that is not yet known what,
    I cannot name; 'tis nameless woe, I wot.   40

Enter GREEN

GREEN: God save your majesty, and well met, gentlemen.
    I hope the King is not yet shipped for Ireland.
QUEEN ISABEL: Why hopest thou so? 'Tis better hope he is,

46–7   *That . . . hope.* The iteration of 'hope', ll. 42–7, is concluded here
with the quibbling 'hope'–'despair'–'hope'.

46   *retired his power*, drawn back his forces.

49   *repeals*, recalls from exile.

50   *uplifted*, raised in rebellion.

57   *all . . . faction*, all the rest of the revolted faction.

59   *staff*, staff of office as steward of the royal household.

62–6   *thou . . . joined.* See ll. 10, 34–40 for the imagery.

63   *dismal heir*, ill-omened offspring.

64   *prodigy*, (a) omen, (b) monstrous birth.

66   *Have . . . joined.* The Queen cannot rejoice at the delivery after
her labour for the child is a monstrous creature that adds to her
suffering.

69   *cozening*, cheating, deceiving.

72   *lingers in extremity*, prolongs at the moment of death.

For his designs crave haste, his haste good hope.
Then wherefore dost thou hope he is not shipped?
GREEN: That he, our hope, might have retired his power,
  And driven into despair an enemy's hope,
  Who strongly hath set footing in this land.
  The banished Bolingbroke repeals himself,
  And with uplifted arms is safe arrived   50
  At Ravenspurgh.
QUEEN ISABEL: Now God in heaven forbid.
GREEN: Ah madam, 'tis too true; and, that is worse,
  The Lord Northumberland, his son young Henry Percy,
  The Lords of Ross, Beaumont, and Willoughby,
  With all their powerful friends are fled to him.
BUSHY: Why have you not proclaimed Northumberland
  And all the rest revolted faction traitors?
GREEN: We have; whereupon the Earl of Worcester
  Hath broken his staff, resigned his stewardship,
  And all the household servants fled with him   60
  To Bolingbroke.
QUEEN ISABEL: So Green, thou art the midwife to my woe,
  And Bolingbroke my sorrow's dismal heir.
  Now hath my soul brought forth her prodigy,
  And I, a gasping new-delivered mother,
  Have woe to woe, sorrow to sorrow joined.
BUSHY: Despair not madam.
QUEEN ISABEL: Who shall hinder me?
  I will despair, and be at enmity
  With cozening hope. He is a flatterer,
  A parasite, a keeper-back of death,   70
  Who gently would dissolve the bands of life,
  Which false hope lingers in extremity.

Enter YORK

GREEN: Here comes the Duke of York.

74   *With . . . neck*, i.e. a collar of mail armour called a gorget which was sometimes worn with civilian dress.

75   *careful business*, anxious matters.

76   *comfortable*, comforting.

79   *crosses*, troubles.

84   *sick . . . surfeit*, i.e. the disastrous time brought about by Richard's extravagant behaviour. See *King Lear*, 'when we are sick in fortune,—often the surfeit of our own behaviour' (I. ii. 129–30).

85   *try*, put to the test.

86   *your son*. Aumerle had gone to Richard in Ireland.

88   *they are cold* Q, F. Some omit 'they are'. *cold*, hostile, indifferent.

91   *presently*, immediately

92   *take my ring*, i.e. as proof that he is sent by York.

97   *An . . . died*. Shakespeare brings forward to an effective moment the Duchess's death which took place three months later.

98–   *God . . . do*. Is York—flustered, senile, incapable, faced with the
100 impossible, helpless, pitiful, human, pragmatic?

101   *So . . . it*, as long as it was not because of disloyalty on my part.

105   *sister*. York's mind still dwells on the death of the Duchess.

QUEEN ISABEL: With signs of war about his aged neck.
　O full of careful business are his looks.
　Uncle, for God's sake speak comfortable words.
YORK: Should I do so I should belie my thoughts.
　Comfort's in heaven, and we are on the earth,
　Where nothing lives but crosses, cares, and grief.
　Your husband, he is gone to save far off,　　　　　　　80
　Whilst others come to make him lose at home.
　Here am I left to underprop his land,
　Who weak with age cannot support myself.
　Now comes the sick hour that his surfeit made,
　Now shall he try his friends that flattered him.

Enter a SERVANT

SERVANT: My lord, your son was gone before I came.
YORK: He was? Why, so. Go all which way it will.
　The nobles they are fled, the commons they are cold,
　And will, I fear, revolt on Herford's side.
　Sirrah, get thee to Pleshey to my sister Gloucester,　　90
　Bid her send me presently a thousand pound—
　Hold, take my ring.
SERVANT: My lord, I had forgot to tell your lordship.
　Today as I came by I called there—
　But I shall grieve you to report the rest.
YORK: What is't, knave?
SERVANT: An hour before I came the Duchess died.
YORK: God for his mercy, what a tide of woes
　Comes rushing on this woeful land at once!
　I know not what to do. I would to God,　　　　　　　100
　So my untruth had not provoked him to it,
　The King had cut off my head with my brother's.
　What, are there no posts dispatched for Ireland?
　How shall we do for money for these wars?
　Come, sister—cousin, I would say—pray pardon me.

111– *Both . . . right.* York's scruples and sense of fairness present him
15 with a dilemma.

117 *dispose of*, make arrangements for.

126–7 *our . . . King*, the King's close affection for us is matched by the
close hatred of those who have no affection for him.

132 *If . . . we*, if the commons are our judges, we too are doomed.

136 *office*, service.
137 *hateful*, full of hate.

Go fellow, get thee home, provide some carts,
And bring away the armour that is there.
Gentlemen, will you go muster men?
If I know how or which way to order these affairs
Thus disorderly thrust into my hands,   110
Never believe me. Both are my kinsmen.
Th one is my sovereign, whom both my oath
And duty bids defend. Th other again
Is my kinsman, whom the King hath wronged,
Whom conscience and my kindred bids to right.
Well, somewhat we must do. Come, cousin,
I'll dispose of you. Gentlemen, go muster up your men,
And meet me presently at Berkeley.
I should to Pleshey, too,
But time will not permit. All is uneven,   120
And everything is left at six and seven.

                      [Exeunt York and the Queen

BUSHY: The wind sits fair for news to go for Ireland,
  But none returns. For us to levy power
  Proportionable to the enemy
  Is all unpossible.
GREEN: Besides, our nearness to the King in love
  Is near the hate of those love not the King.
BAGOT: And that's the wavering commons, for their love
  Lies in their purses, and whoso empties them
  By so much fills their hearts with deadly hate.   130
BUSHY: Wherein the King stands generally condemned.
BAGOT: If judgment lie in them, then so do we,
  Because we ever have been near the King.
GREEN: Well I will for refuge straight to Bristol Castle.
  The Earl of Wiltshire is already there.
BUSHY: Thither will I with you; for little office
  Will the hateful commons perform for us,

140   *I . . . majesty.* There is some confusion over Bagot. He does not join Richard (III. ii. 122). In II. iii. 164 he is reported at Bristol Castle with Bushy and others, but he is not mentioned when Bushy and Green are sent to execution. He reappears in IV. 1. to testify against Aumerle with evidence that is self-contradictory.

141   *presages*, forebodings.

143   *That's . . . Bolingbroke*, that's according to York's success in defeating Bolingbroke.

145   *Is . . . dry.* Proverbial.

Bushy to comfort the Queen takes the common-sense view of King Lear, 'nothing will come of nothing', and asserts that her forebodings are shadows, illusions, nothings. The Queen replies with a popular contemporary paradox that nothing not only implies something but is here actually something, though unknown, unborn, and nameless. Her condition is not caused by the illusions created by melancholy, but by the self-generation of something from nothing. For a similar notion see Sonnet 136 where the poet addresses his love, 'For nothing hold me, so it please thee hold That nothing me, a something sweet to thee'. There is an analogy with the perspective paintings (ll. 18–20) which Bushy has not perceived.

Richard's actions in II. i and reports of Bolingbroke's quick response are here reflected in emotions.

The Queen's premonitions give way to despair; York's confusion and dilemma make him wish for death; the favourites depart but with a sense of doom.

Gloucestershire

The opening speeches give the impression of movement until the speakers arrive before Berkeley Castle.

5   *Draws.* A singular verb with a plural subject occurs elsewhere (II. i. 252). Here it may be that the 'hills' and 'ways' are thought of as one general characteristic.

6–16   *And . . . enjoyed.* Is this—fawning, flattery, true of Bolingbroke's conversation, evidence of Bolingbroke's charisma? See I. iv. 24–36.

Except like curs to tear us all to pieces.
Will you go along with us?
BAGOT: No, I will to Ireland to his majesty. 140
Farewell. If heart's presages be not vain,
We three here part that ne'er shall meet again.
BUSHY: That's as York thrives to beat back Bolingbroke.
GREEN: Alas poor Duke, the task he undertakes
Is numbering sands, and drinking oceans dry.
Where one on his side fights, thousands will fly.
BAGOT: Farewell at once, for once, for all, and ever.
BUSHY: Well, we may meet again.
BAGOT: I fear me never.   [*Exeunt*

SCENE THREE

Enter BOLINGBROKE *and* NORTHUMBERLAND

BOLINGBROKE: How far is it, my lord, to Berkeley now?
NORTHUMBERLAND: Believe me noble lord,
I am a stranger here in Gloucestershire.
These high wild hills and rough uneven ways
Draws out our miles, and makes them wearisome.
And yet your fair discourse hath been as sugar,
Making the hard way sweet and delectable.
But I bethink me what a weary way

9   *Cotswold.* Q 'Cotshall'.

11   *beguiled,* passed easily.
12   *tediousness and process,* wearisome course.

15   *in joy,* enjoyable.
16   *enjoyed.* A quibble on 'in joy' (l. 15). *By this,* i.e. the anticipation of enjoying Bolingbroke's conversation.

21   *young Harry Percy.* Known as Hotspur. Shakespeare makes him a 'boy' (l. 36) whereas historically he was two years older than Bolingbroke. Why? In *1 Henry IV* he rebels against Henry (Bolingbroke) and is killed at the battle of Shrewsbury in 1403.

36   *Have . . . boy?* Percy has so far ignored Bolingbroke, and Northumberland speaks sharply.

From Ravenspurgh to Cotswold will be found
In Ross and Willoughby, wanting your company,   10
Which I protest hath very much beguiled
The tediousness and process of my travel.
But theirs is sweetened with the hope to have
The present benefit which I possess;
And hope to joy is little less in joy
Than hope enjoyed. By this the weary lords
Shall make their way seem short as mine hath done
By sight of what I have, your noble company.
BOLINGBROKE: Of much less value is my company
Than your good words. But who comes here?   20

Enter HARRY PERCY

NORTHUMBERLAND: It is my son young Harry Percy,
Sent from my brother Worcester whencesoever.
Harry, how fares your uncle?
PERCY: I had thought my lord to have learned his health of you.
NORTHUMBERLAND: Why, is he not with the Queen?
PERCY: No my good lord, he hath forsook the court,
Broken his staff of office, and dispersed
The household of the King.
NORTHUMBERLAND: What was his reason?
He was not so resolved when last we spake together.
PERCY: Because your lordship was proclaimed traitor.   30
But he my lord is gone to Ravenspurgh
To offer service to the Duke of Herford,
And sent me over by Berkeley to discover
What power the Duke of York had levied there,
Then with directions to repair to Ravenspurgh.
NORTHUMBERLAND: Have you forgot the Duke of Herford,
    boy?
PERCY: No my good lord, for that is not forgot
Which ne'er I did remember. To my knowledge

42   *tender*. The pun is a modest disclaimer.

43–4   *Which . . . desert*. Ironical, assuming the audience knows of the future events, the theme of *1 Henry IV*.

45–50   *I . . . it*. See *1 Henry IV*, I. iii. 241–54, for Hotspur's bitter recollection of this 'candy deal of courtesy'.

47   *As . . . remembering*, as having a heart that remembers.

49   *still*, always.

61   *unfelt thanks*, i.e. gratitude without tangible rewards. *which*, i.e. treasury.

65   *Evermore . . . poor*, thanks are always the only treasure store of the poor.

66   *to years*, of age.

67   *Stands . . . bounty*, represents all I have to bestow.

I never in my life did look on him.

NORTHUMBERLAND: Then learn to know him now. This is
    the Duke.   40

PERCY: My gracious lord, I tender you my service,
Such as it is, being tender, raw, and young,
Which elder days shall ripen and confirm
To more approved service and desert.

BOLINGBROKE: I thank thee gentle Percy, and be sure
I count myself in nothing else so happy
As in a soul remembering my good friends;
And as my fortune ripens with thy love,
It shall be still thy true love's recompense.
My heart this covenant makes, my hand thus seals it.   50

NORTHUMBERLAND: How far is it to Berkeley, and what stir
Keeps good old York there with his men of war?

PERCY: There stands the castle by yon tuft of trees,
Manned with three hundred men, as I have heard,
And in it are the Lords of York, Berkeley, and Seymour,
None else of name and noble estimate.

Enter ROSS *and* WILLOUGHBY

NORTHUMBERLAND: Here comes the Lords of Ross and
    Willoughby,
Bloody with spurring, fiery red with haste.

BOLINGBROKE: Welcome my lords. I wot your love pursues
A banished traitor. All my treasury   60
Is yet but unfelt thanks, which more enriched
Shall be your love and labour's recompense.

ROSS: Your presence makes us rich, most noble lord.

WILLOUGHBY: And far surmounts our labour to attain it.

BOLINGBROKE: Evermore thank's the exchequer of the poor,
Which till my infant fortune comes to years
Stands for my bounty. But who comes here?

70 *my . . . 'Lancaster'*, I answer only to the title Lancaster.

75 *raze*, erase. Q 'race' perhaps glances at 'race'=root out. See *Macbeth*, V. iii. 42. *title*. A pun on 'title' and 'tittle', jot.

78 *pricks*, spurs, urges.
79 *absent time*, time of Richard's absence.
80 *self-borne*, carried for your own ends. Some see a quibble on 'self-born' in opposition to 'native'.

84 *duty*, i.e. the act of kneeling. *deceivable*, deceitful.

86 *Tut, tut*. Some consider this extra-metrical exclamation an actor's addition.
87–8 *that . . . profane*. The religious connotation of grace, 'heavenly grace', common to Elizabethans, makes this a severe rebuke.

90 *dust*, speck.

94 *despised*, despicable.

Act Two, Scene Three

Enter BERKELEY

NORTHUMBERLAND: It is my Lord of Berkeley, as I guess.
BERKELEY: My Lord of Herford, my message is to you.
BOLINGBROKE: My lord, my answer is to 'Lancaster'.   70
  And I am come to seek that name in England,
  And I must find that title in your tongue
  Before I make reply to aught you say.
BERKELEY: Mistake me not my lord. 'Tis not my meaning
  To raze one title of your honour out.
  To you my lord I come, what lord you will,
  From the most gracious regent of this land,
  The Duke of York, to know what pricks you on
  To take advantage of the absent time,
  And fright our native peace with self-borne arms.   80

Enter YORK

BOLINGBROKE: I shall not need transport my words by you,
  Here comes his grace in person. My noble uncle.

                                                    [*Kneels*
YORK: Show me thy humble heart, and not thy knee,
  Whose duty is deceivable and false.
BOLINGBROKE: My gracious uncle—
YORK: Tut, tut, grace me no grace, nor uncle me no uncle.
  I am no traitor's uncle, and that word 'grace'
  In an ungracious mouth is but profane.
  Why have those banished and forbidden legs
  Dared once to touch a dust of England's ground?   90
  But then more 'why'—why have they dared to march
  So many miles upon her peaceful bosom,
  Frighting her pale-faced villages with war,
  And ostentation of despised arms?
  Comest thou because the anointed King is hence?
  Why, foolish boy, the King is left behind,

98   *lord . . . youth*, in the full vigour of youth.
99–   *As . . . French.* Such an incident has not been discovered else-
101   where.

103   *palsy*, paralysis, or perhaps the feebleness of age.

106   *condition*, personal quality.
107   *condition*, circumstance.

111   *braving*, defiant.

113   *for*, on behalf of.

115   *indifferent*, impartial.

119   *royalties*, privileges granted by a king.
120   *arms*, (a) possession, (b) coat of arms.
121   *unthrifts*, spendthrifts, i.e. Bushy, Bagot, and Green.

127   *rouse*, flush out (game). *to the bay*, until the quarry turns at bay.
128   *denied to sue*, refused the right to sue for. *livery*, legal delivery of
       property into a person's possession.
129   *letters patents*, open letter from a king or other high authority
       granting rights or privileges.

And in my loyal bosom lies his power.
Were I but now lord of such hot youth
As when brave Gaunt, thy father, and myself
Rescued the Black Prince, that young Mars of men,   100
From forth the ranks of many thousand French,
O then how quickly should this arm of mine,
Now prisoner to the palsy, chastise thee,
And minister correction to thy fault.

BOLINGBROKE: My gracious uncle, let me know my fault.
On what condition stands it and wherein?

YORK: Even in condition of the worst degree,
In gross rebellion and detested treason.
Thou art a banished man, and here art come
Before the expiration of thy time   110
In braving arms against thy sovereign.

BOLINGBROKE: As I was banished, I was banished Herford;
But as I come, I come for Lancaster.
And noble uncle I beseech your grace
Look on my wrongs with an indifferent eye.
You are my father, for methinks in you
I see old Gaunt alive. O then my father,
Will you permit that I shall stand condemned
A wandering vagabond, my rights and royalties
Plucked from my arms perforce, and given away   120
To upstart unthrifts? Wherefore was I born?
If that my cousin King be King in England,
It must be granted I am Duke of Lancaster.
You have a son, Aumerle, my noble cousin.
Had you first died, and he been thus trod down,
He should have found his uncle Gaunt a father
To rouse his wrongs and chase them to the bay.
I am denied to sue my livery here,
And yet my letters patents give me leave.

130   *distrained*, seized by officers of the king.
131   *and all*, and everything else.

133   *challenge law*, demand justice.

135   *inheritance . . . descent*, inheritance by unblemished descent.

137   *It . . . upon*, it is your grace's obligation.
138   *endowments*, i.e. things which properly belong to him or his
       possessions (which have been bestowed upon them).

142   *kind*, way, manner.
143   *Be . . . carver*, help himself (a) at table, (b) by force of arms. See
       Hamlet, I. iii. 20, 'Carve for himself'.
144   *To . . . wrong*, to attain the right by wrongful means.

147–   *The . . . oath*. See III. iii. 196. Is there any ambiguity in 'his own',
  50   or is this a true statement of the position at this time? See
       1 Henry IV, IV. iii. 60–88.

153   *ill-left*, left unprepared.

155   *attach*, arrest.

158   *as neuter*, neutral. York, the conciliator, compromises here since
       he is powerless to do anything else.

My father's goods are all distrained and sold,   130
And these, and all, are all amiss employed.
What would you have me do? I am a subject,
And I challenge law. Attorneys are denied me,
And therefore personally I lay my claim
To my inheritance of free descent.
NORTHUMBERLAND: The noble Duke hath been too much
    abused.
ROSS: It stands your grace upon to do him right.
WILLOUGHBY: Base men by his endowments are made great.
YORK: My lords of England, let me tell you this: 140
    I have had feeling of my cousin's wrongs,
    And laboured all I could to do him right.
    But in this kind to come, in braving arms,
    Be his own carver, and cut out his way,
    To find our right with wrong—it may not be.
    And you that do abet him in this kind
    Cherish rebellion, and are rebels all.
NORTHUMBERLAND: The noble Duke hath sworn his coming is
    But for his own, and for the right of that
    We all have strongly sworn to give him aid.
    And let him never see joy that breaks that oath.   150
YORK: Well well, I see the issue of these arms.
    I cannot mend it, I must needs confess,
    Because my power is weak and all ill-left.
    But if I could, by Him that gave me life,
    I would attach you all, and make you stoop
    Unto the sovereign mercy of the King.
    But since I cannot, be it known unto you
    I do remain as neuter. So fare you well,
    Unless you please to enter in the castle,
    And there repose you for this night.   160
BOLINGBROKE: An offer, uncle, that we will accept;
    But we must win your grace to go with us

165–6 *The . . . away.* Is this consistent with ll. 112–35 and ll. 147–8?
165   *caterpillars . . . commonwealth*, parasites on the kingdom.
166   *weed.* See note to III. iv. 37–9.

170   *Things . . . care.* York justifies his inaction with the proverb 'past
       cure, past care'. Is he—a comic figure, time-server, too honest,
       unfit for his post, reasonable, peacemaker?

Wales

S.D.   *Welsh Captain.* In Holinshed he is Owen Glendower.

2   *hardly*, with difficulty.

8–15   *The . . . kings.* For a similar Welsh susceptibility to omens and
       withdrawal from action, see *1 Henry IV*, III. i. 1–43, IV. iv. 16–18.
8   *The . . . withered.* As bays were the emblems of victory and
       immortality their withering was regarded as ominous.
9   *And . . . heaven.* Frequency of meteor showers was regarded as
       foretelling changes in kingdoms.
10   *looks . . . on*, (a) appears, (b) casts its harmful influence on.
11   *lean-looked*, lean looking. Is this through too much study by
       night? See *Julius Cæsar*, I. ii. 194–5, 'Yond Cassius has a lean and
       hungry look; He thinks too much'. *prophets*, soothsayers.
14   *to enjoy*, in the hope of enjoying.

To Bristol Castle, which they say is held
By Bushy, Bagot, and their complices,
The caterpillars of the commonwealth,
Which I have sworn to weed and pluck away.
YORK: It may be I will go with you; but yet I'll pause,
For I am loath to break our country's laws.
Nor friends, nor foes, to me welcome you are.
Things past redress are now with me past care.   170
                                        [*Exeunt*

SCENE FOUR

Enter EARL OF SALISBURY *and a* WELSH CAPTAIN

CAPTAIN: My Lord of Salisbury, we have stayed ten days
And hardly kept our countrymen together,
And yet we hear no tidings from the King
Therefore we will disperse ourselves. Farewell.
SALISBURY: Stay yet another day, thou trusty Welshman.
The King reposeth all his confidence in thee.
CAPTAIN: 'Tis thought the King is dead. We will not stay.
The bay trees in our country are all withered,
And meteors fright the fixed stars of heaven.
The pale-faced moon looks bloody on the earth,   10
And lean-looked prophets whisper fearful change;
Rich men look sad, and ruffians dance and leap,
The one in fear to lose what they enjoy,
The other to enjoy by rage and war.
These signs forerun the death or fall of kings.
Farewell. Our countrymen are gone and fled,
As well assured Richard their king is dead.   [*Exit*
SALISBURY: Ah Richard! With the eyes of heavy mind

19–21 I . . . west. See III. iii. 178–83 for similar imagery.

22 Witnessing, foretelling.

24 crossly, adversely.

The withdrawal of the Welsh influenced by omens, and Salisbury's premonition following York's neutralization emphasize the unfavourable turn of Richard's fortunes. While there were sceptics, the attitude of the authorities after the 1575 earthquake and a Privy Council order (1580) to Archbishop Grindal enforcing prayers in churches show that unusual phenomena were represented as direct signs from God.

I see thy glory like a shooting star
Fall to the base earth from the firmament.   20
Thy sun sets weeping in the lowly west,
Witnessing storms to come, woe, and unrest.
Thy friends are fled to wait upon thy foes,
And crossly to thy good all fortune goes.   [*Exit*

Bristol

S.D.   Percy, Ross, and Willoughby added in F, which makes a more impressive presentation.

3   *presently*, immediately. *part*, part from.

4   *With . . . lives,* with over-stressing the wickedness of your lives.

5–6   *to . . . hands.* Is there any significance in Bolingbroke's allusion to Pilate's rejection of responsibility for Christ's death? Is he unconsciously identifying himself with Pilate? See IV. i. 238–41.

9   *happy,* fortunate. *blood and lineaments,* birth and personal features —perhaps royal presence. See III. iii. 68–70.

11   *in manner,* as it were. *hours.* Is a quibble intended with 'whores' as in *As You Like It,* II. vii. 24–8?

12   *Made . . . him.* Nothing elsewhere in the play substantiates this. Holinshed does accuse Richard of adultery.

13   *Broke . . . bed,* i.e. broke the marital relations between Richard and the Queen.

20   *sighed . . . clouds,* i.e. added to, as well as being in the midst of, foreign clouds. See *Romeo and Juliet,* I. i. 127, 'Adding to clouds more clouds with his deep sighs'.

22   *fed . . . signories,* swallowed up my estates.

23   *Disparked my parks,* turned to other uses my game preserves.

ACT THREE

SCENE ONE

Enter BOLINGBROKE, YORK, NORTHUMBERLAND, PERCY, ROSS, WILLOUGHBY, *with* BUSHY *and* GREEN, *prisoners*

BOLINGBROKE: Bring forth these men.
Bushy and Green, I will not vex your souls,
Since presently your souls must part your bodies,
With too much urging your pernicious lives,
For 'twere no charity; yet to wash your blood
From off my hands, here in the view of men
I will unfold some causes of your deaths.
You have misled a prince, a royal king,
A happy gentleman in blood and lineaments,
By you unhappied and disfigured clean.   10
You have in manner with your sinful hours
Made a divorce betwixt his Queen and him,
Broke the possession of a royal bed,
And stained the beauty of a fair queen's cheeks
With tears, drawn from her eyes by your foul wrongs.
Myself a prince by fortune of my birth,
Near to the King in blood, and near in love
Till you did make him misinterpret me,
Have stooped my neck under your injuries,
And sighed my English breath in foreign clouds,   20
Eating the bitter bread of banishment
Whilst you have fed upon my signories,
Disparked my parks, and felled my forest woods,

24   *From . . . coat*, i.e. torn from the cames the stained glass of my
      family coat-of-arms.
25   *Razed . . . imprese*, erased my crest. *imprese*. The *impresa* was a
      small emblematic design or picture with a motto devised for,
      and worn by, noblemen and their retainers.
          The defacing of a nobleman's coat-of-arms was regarded as a
      particularly heinous crime.
28–34 *This . . . hell.* Bolingbroke condemns Bushy and Green to death
      without trial. Are his reasons adequate or is his action unjust? In
      Henry V the conspirators are surrendered to 'the answer of the
      law' and all three make a confession of guilt. Is it significant that
      Bushy and Green make no confession and foretell trouble for
      Bolingbroke claiming that he is unjust?

35   *dispatched*, executed.

36   *your house*. At Langley, Buckinghamshire.
37   *intreated*, treated.

41   *at large*, in general terms.

43   *Glendower*. Perhaps the Welsh spokesman in II. iv. Glendower
      was a well-known leader of the Welsh against whom Boling-
      broke as king campaigned in the following year.
          In *1 Henry IV* Harry Percy accuses King Henry (Bolingbroke)
      of stepping 'a little higher than his vow' 'but to be Duke of
      Lancaster' by taking action against abuses, and of proceeding
      'further, cut me off the heads Of all the favourites that the absent
      king In deputation left behind him here' (IV. iii. 60–87). Is there
      justification for Henry's sincerity in his patriotic concern?

Near Barkloughly Castle

1   *Barkloughly*. The modern Harlech.
2   *brooks*, enjoys.

From my own windows torn my household coat,
Razed out my imprese, leaving me no sign
Save men's opinions and my living blood
To show the world I am a gentleman.
This and much more, much more than twice all this,
Condemns you to the death. See them delivered over
To execution and the hand of death.   30
BUSHY: More welcome is the stroke of death to me
   Than Bolingbroke to England. Lords farewell.
GREEN: My comfort is that heaven will take our souls,
   And plague injustice with the pains of hell.
BOLINGBROKE: My Lord Northumberland, see them
   dispatched.
               [*Exit Northumberland with Bushy and Green*
Uncle, you say the Queen is at your house.
For God's sake fairly let her be intreated.
Tell her I send to her my kind commends.
Take special care my greetings be delivered.
YORK: A gentleman of mine I have dispatched   40
   With letters of your love to her at large.
BOLINGBROKE: Thanks, gentle uncle. Come lords, away,
   To fight with Glendower and his complices.
   A while to work, and after holiday.   [*Exeunt*

SCENE TWO

Drums; flourish and colours. Enter KING RICHARD, AUMERLE,
   the BISHOP OF CARLISLE, *and soldiers*

KING RICHARD: Barkloughly Castle call they this at hand?
AUMERLE: Yea my lord. How brooks your grace the air
   After your late tossing on the breaking seas?

6   *salute.* What gesture is apt? See l. 11.

8   *long-parted mother with,* mother long parted from.

9   *fondly,* foolishly emotional. *tears and smiles.* Shakespeare frequently refers to these confused emotions. See V. ii. 32; *King Lear,* IV. iii. 20; *Winter's Tale,* V. ii. 50.

11   *And . . . hands.* Is he bestowing a blessing?

13   *sense,* desire, appetite.

14   *spiders . . . venom.* Spiders have poisonous fangs. They were sometimes called 'attercops' = poison-cups, in Shakespeare's day.

15   *heavy-gaited,* clumsy moving. *toads,* i.e. also poisonous creatures.

20   *a lurking adder.* The snake hidden in the grass or under a flower had become a proverbial expression of warning from Virgil's *Eclogue* III, l. 93, 'Latet anguis in herba'.

21   *double . . . touch.* The snake's forked tongue was believed to be poisonous.

23   *senseless conjuration,* entreaty to things without human senses.

       Are the lords mocking him or not? Is Richard's invocation—naïve, childlike, effeminate, sentimental, priest-like, inspired, maudlin, fantasied?

24-5   *these . . . soldiers.* Perhaps an echo of *Luke,* xix. 40, 'I tell you, that if these would hold their peace, then shall the stones cry immediately'. Further echoes may come from the two accounts of the sowing of the dragon's teeth by Cadmus and later by Jason, from which sprang up armed men who fought 'a family conflict' among themselves—in the latter story they were provoked by a stone thrown by Jason to save himself. (Ovid, *Metamorphoses,* III and VII.)

27   *Fear,* doubt.

29-32 *The . . . redress,* we must accept, not neglect, the help that heaven offers; otherwise in disobeying the will of heaven, we refuse heaven's offer, the means of saving the kingdom and restoring our power. Not in F.

KING RICHARD: Needs must I like it well. I weep for joy
  To stand upon my kingdom once again.
  Dear earth I do salute thee with my hand,
  Though rebels wound thee with their horses' hoofs.
  As a long-parted mother with her child
  Plays fondly with her tears and smiles in meeting,
  So weeping, smiling, greet I thee my earth,   10
  And do thee favours with my royal hands.
  Feed not thy sovereign's foe, my gentle earth,
  Nor with thy sweets comfort his ravenous sense,
  But let thy spiders that suck up thy venom,
  And heavy-gaited toads lie in their way,
  Doing annoyance to the treacherous feet,
  Which with usurping steps do trample thee.
  Yield stinging nettles to mine enemies;
  And when they from thy bosom pluck a flower,
  Guard it, I pray thee, with a lurking adder,   20
  Whose double tongue may with a mortal touch
  Throw death upon thy sovereign's enemies.
  Mock not my senseless conjuration lords.
  This earth shall have a feeling, and these stones
  Prove armed soldiers ere her native king
  Shall falter under foul rebellion's arms.
BISHOP OF CARLISLE: Fear not my lord, that power that
    made you king
  Hath power to keep you king in spite of all.
  The means that heavens yield must be embraced
  And not neglected; else heaven would,   30
  And we will not—heaven's offer we refuse,
  The proffered means of succour and redress.

33   *remiss*, neglectful.

34   *security*, complacent confidence, over-confidence.

36   *Discomfortable*, disheartening.

37-8 *when . . . world*, when the sun, that lights the other side of the world, is set.

38   *and*. Q, F 'that'.

42   *fires*, illumines.

46   *at themselves*, at the exposure of their sins.

47-53 *So . . . sin*. Richard continues his image as the sun. One of his badges was the sun in splendour, another was the sunburst.

49   *Whilst . . . Antipodes*. Not in F. Richard was of course in Ireland, but the sun was shining on the people at the other side of the world.

55   *balm*, consecrated oil.

56   *depose*. Again the ominous word.

58   *pressed*, forced into service, conscripted.

59   *shrewd*, (a) accursed, (b) harmful.

59-61 *golden . . . angel*. What effect is intended by the punning on 'golden crown'–'heavenly pay'–'glorious angel'? 'Crown' and 'angel' were coins.

60-2 *God . . . right*. See *Matt.*, xxvi. 53. Is Richard likening himself to Christ, or is he adopting Satan's suggestion? (*Matt.*, iv. 6.)

63   *power*, army.

AUMERLE: He means my lord that we are too remiss,
  Whilst Bolingbroke through our security
  Grows strong and great in substance and in power.
KING RICHARD: Discomfortable cousin knowest thou not
  That when the searching eye of heaven is hid
  Behind the globe, and lights the lower world,
  Then thieves and robbers range abroad unseen
  In murders and in outrage boldly here;   40
  But when from under this terrestrial ball
  He fires the proud tops of the eastern pines,
  And darts his light through every guilty hole,
  Then murders, treasons, and detested sins,
  The cloak of night being plucked from off their backs,
  Stand bare and naked, trembling at themselves?
  So when this thief, this traitor Bolingbroke,
  Who all this while hath revelled in the night,
  Whilst we were wandering with the Antipodes,
  Shall see us rising in our throne the east,   50
  His treasons will sit blushing in his face,
  Not able to endure the sight of day,
  But self-affrighted, tremble at his sin.
  Not all the water in the rough rude sea
  Can wash the balm off from an anointed king.
  The breath of worldly men cannot depose
  The deputy elected by the Lord.
  For every man that Bolingbroke hath pressed
  To lift shrewd steel against our golden crown,
  God for his Richard hath in heavenly pay   60
  A glorious angel. Then if angels fight,
  Weak men must fall for heaven still guards the right.

Enter SALISBURY

KING RICHARD: Welcome my lord. How far off lies your
  power?

64   *near*, nearer.

69   *O . . . return*. Proverbial.

76–81   *But . . . pride*. These lines have the rhyme pattern of the sestet of a
        Shakespearian sonnet, an intensely emotional image complement-
        ing, sonnet-like, Salisbury's lines 'One . . . fled'.

76–9   *But . . . dead*. There is some evidence that Richard had a rosy face
        given to quick flushes and sudden pallor.

79   *dead*, death-like.

84   *coward* Q. F 'sluggard'.

88   *high*, i.e. in courage and authority.

90   s.d. *Scroop*. Sir Stephen Scroop not Sir William Scroop, the Earl
        of Wiltshire. See l. 122. Stephen Scroop was a loyal supporter of
        Richard.

92   *care-tuned*, tuned to the mode of sorrow. *deliver*, express to.

93–   *Mine . . . day*. Is Richard—pious, patient, resolute, sensible,
103   enduring, stoical, acquiescent, resigned, spiritless, undaunted?

SALISBURY: Nor near nor farther off, my gracious lord,
   Than this weak arm. Discomfort guides my tongue
   And bids me speak of nothing but despair.
   One day too late, I fear me, noble lord,
   Hath clouded all thy happy days on earth.
   O call back yesterday, bid time return,
   And thou shalt have twelve thousand fighting men.   70
   Today, today, unhappy day too late,
   O'erthrows thy joys, friends, fortune, and thy state;
   For all the Welshmen, hearing thou wert dead,
   Are gone to Bolingbroke, dispersed and fled.
AUMERLE: Comfort my liege, why looks your grace so pale?
KING RICHARD: But now the blood of twenty thousand men
   Did triumph in my face, and they are fled.
   And till so much blood thither come again,
   Have I not reason to look pale and dead?
   All souls that will be safe fly from my side,   80
   For time hath set a blot upon my pride.
AUMERLE: Comfort my liege, remember who you are.
KING RICHARD: I had forgot myself, am I not King?
   Awake thou coward majesty; thou sleepest.
   Is not the King's name twenty thousand names?
   Arm, arm, my name, a puny subject strikes
   At thy great glory. Look not to the ground,
   Ye favourites of a King, are we not high?
   High be our thoughts. I know my uncle York
   Hath power enough to serve our turn. But who comes
      here?   90

Enter SCROOP

SCROOP: More health and happiness betide my liege
   Than can my care-tuned tongue deliver him.
KING RICHARD: Mine ear is open and my heart prepared.
   The worst is worldly loss thou canst unfold.

95   *care*, trouble, burden.

99   *fellow*, equal.

101   *They . . . us*, i.e. because the King is God's deputy.
102   *Cry*, although you may cry out.

109   *his limits*, its banks.

113   *women's*, unbrokèn.
114   *big*, i.e. men's tones. *female*, weak.
115   *arms*, armour.
116   *beadsmen*, almsmen, pensioners who had the duty of offering prayers for their benefactor.
117   *double-fatal yew*. The leaves and berries are poisonous and bows were made from the wood.
118   *distaff-women*, women whose work is spinning. *rusty bills*. A bill had a curved blade or a spiked axe-head at the end of a wooden shaft. These were rusty from disuse.
119   *seat*, throne.
122   *Where is Bagot?* See note to II. ii. 140.

125   *Measure*, pass through. *peaceful*, unopposed.

128   *Peace . . . indeed*. Grim irony. See *Macbeth*, IV. iii. 178–9.

Say, is my kingdom lost? Why, 'twas my care,
And what loss is it to be rid of care?
Strives Bolingbroke to be as great as we?
Greater he shall not be. If he serve God,
We'll serve Him too, and be his fellow so.
Revolt our subjects? That we cannot mend;   100
They break their faith to God as well as us.
Cry woe, destruction, ruin, and decay.
The worst is death, and death will have his day.
SCROOP: Glad am I that your highness is so armed
  To bear the tidings of calamity.
  Like an unseasonable stormy day
  Which makes the silver rivers drown their shores,
  As if the world were all dissolved to tears;
  So high above his limits swells the rage
  Of Bolingbroke, covering your fearful land   110
  With hard bright steel, and hearts harder than steel.
  Whitebeards have armed their thin and hairless scalps
  Against thy majesty; boys with women's voices
  Strive to speak big and clap their female joints
  In stiff unwieldy arms against thy crown;
  Thy very beadsmen learn to bend their bows
  Of double-fatal yew against thy state;
  Yea distaff-women manage rusty bills
  Against thy seat; both young and old rebel,
  And all goes worse than I have power to tell.   120
KING RICHARD: Too well, too well thou tellest a tale so ill.
  Where is the Earl of Wiltshire? Where is Bagot?
  What is become of Bushy, where is Green,
  That they have let the dangerous enemy
  Measure our confines with such peaceful steps?
  If we prevail, their heads shall pay for it.
  I warrant they have made peace with Bolingbroke.
SCROOP: Peace have they made with him indeed, my lord.

129   *vipers . . . redemption.* Perhaps an echo of *Matt.*, xxiii. 33, 'ye generation of vipers, how will ye escape the damnation of hell?'

131   *Snakes . . . heart.* A common image descriptive of traitors. See V. iii. 57.

132   *Three Judases.* Is Richard implying that he is Christ-like, or is this a common epithet for traitors? Perhaps Shakespeare made a slip since Richard does not know until l. 141 that three, not four (ll. 122–3), favourites have been executed.

        Richard rages with unreasonable conclusions.

134   *spotted*, sinful.

135   *his property*, its essential nature.

138   *with hands*, i.e. perhaps by placing hands between the king's hands on taking an oath of loyalty.

141–3   *Is . . . power.* Is Richard involved in any stage business?

144   *comfort.* Is Richard a 'too quick despairer'?

150   *deposed*, dethroned, displaced from office.

153–4 *small . . . bones.* Variously interpreted, but it seems best to take it as referring either to a corpse i.e. our corpse that replica of lifeless earth that is a mere paste-like covering for our bones; or to a grave.

153   *model*, (a) small replica or image, (b) human body (microcosm), (c) a mould.

KING RICHARD: O villains, vipers, damned without
    redemption,
  Dogs easily won to fawn on any man,   130
  Snakes in my heart-blood warmed, that sting my heart;
  Three Judases, each one thrice worse than Judas.
  Would they make peace? Terrible hell
  Make war upon their spotted souls for this.
SCROOP: Sweet love, I see, changing his property,
  Turns to the sourest and most deadly hate.
  Again uncurse their souls; their peace is made
  With heads and not with hands. Those whom you curse
  Have felt the worst of death's destroying wound,
  And lie full low, graved in the hollow ground.   140
AUMERLE: Is Bushy, Green, and the Earl of Wiltshire dead?
SCROOP: Ay, all of them at Bristol lost their heads.
AUMERLE: Where is the Duke my father with his power?
KING RICHARD: No matter where—of comfort no man speak.
  Let's talk of graves, of worms, and epitaphs,
  Make dust our paper, and with rainy eyes
  Write sorrow on the bosom of the earth.
  Let's choose executors and talk of wills.
  And yet not so, for what can we bequeath
  Save our deposed bodies to the ground?   150
  Our lands, our lives, and all are Bolingbroke's,
  And nothing can we call our own but death,
  And that small model of the barren earth
  Which serves as paste and cover to our bones.
  For God's sake let us sit upon the ground

156–   *sad . . . murdered.* The *Mirror for Magistrates* (1559) and its enlarged
60   reissues were collections of such stories as Shakespeare makes
       Richard recall. Historically Richard was much concerned over
       the murder of Edward II whom he sought to have canonized.
       One of the values of history for Elizabethans was to learn how
       to endure misfortunes by recalling the tragedies of others (see
       Ribner, *History and Drama in the Age of Shakespeare*, p. 23).

158   *they,* of those they.

161   *rounds,* encircles.

162   *antic.* Death was frequently represented as a skeleton whose skull
       'grinned'. He was envisaged as clown-like, fooling men with a
       false sense of security. In Holbein's woodcut of Death and the
       Queen, Death wears 'antic' regalia of cap and bells.

163   *state,* majesty.

164   *scene,* i.e. life as a play enacted on a stage.

165   *monarchize,* play the monarch. *kill with looks,* i.e. a mere glance
       from a king could give an order for his execution. Perhaps there
       may be a hint of the fabulous lizard basilisk whose glance was
       supposed to kill. The word basilisk is derived from the Greek
       word for king.

166   *self . . . conceit,* worthless high opinion of himself.

167–8 *flesh . . . impregnable.* Brass was a common emblem of imperish-
       ability (*Measure for Measure*, V. i. 11–13; Sonnet 64). Some see an
       echo of *Job*, vi. 12.

168   *humoured thus,* either death having allowed the king to do as he
       will, or death having amused himself.

170   *castle wall.* A glance back at the 'brass impregnable' which 'walls
       about our life'.

171   *Cover your heads.* Hats were removed in the king's presence,
       otherwise they were worn indoors and outdoors.

171–7 *mock . . . king.* Richard points the distinction between the 'king's
       two bodies' (see Introduction, pp. 10, 14), and insists on his mere
       humanity, a kind of self-deposition. Is he—perceptive, sensitive,
       weak, wavering, indecisive, despairing, rational, imaginative?

176   *Subjected,* (a) at the mercy of (human needs), (b) made into a
       subject, i.e. dethroned.

179   *the . . . wail,* that which leads to lamenting.

183   *to fight,* in fighting.

184–5 *fight . . . breath,* to die fighting is to overcome death by means of
       death, but to fear dying is a slavish submission to death.

And tell sad stories of the death of kings:
How some have been deposed, some slain in war,
Some haunted by the ghosts they have deposed,
Some poisoned by their wives, some sleeping killed,
All murdered. For within the hollow crown   160
That rounds the mortal temples of a king
Keeps death his court; and there the antic sits,
Scoffing his state and grinning at his pomp,
Allowing him a breath, a little scene,
To monarchize, be feared, and kill with looks,
Infusing him with self and vain conceit,
As if this flesh which walls about our life
Were brass impregnable; and humoured thus,
Comes at the last, and with a little pin
Bores through his castle wall, and farewell king!   170
Cover your heads, and mock not flesh and blood
With solemn reverence; throw away respect,
Tradition, form, and ceremonious duty;
For you have but mistook me all this while.
I live with bread like you, feel want,
Taste grief, need friends. Subjected thus,
How can you say to me, I am a king?
BISHOP OF CARLISLE: My lord, wise men ne'er sit and wail
    their woes,
But presently prevent the ways to wail.
To fear the foe, since fear oppresseth strength,   180
Gives in your weakness strength unto your foe,
And so your follies fight against yourself.
Fear, and be slain, no worse can come to fight;
And fight and die is death destroying death,
Where fearing dying pays death servile breath.

186   *of him*, his whereabouts.

189   *change*, exchange. *day of doom*, day that judges between us.
190   *ague*, fever. *overblown*, passed off.

194–7 *Men . . . say*. What is the point of the stanza form?
194   *complexion*, appearance.

198–9 *I . . . spoken*, i.e. like the torturer stretching little by little his
      victims on the rack.

203   *Upon his party*, on his side.

204   *Beshrew*, curse.
204–5 *forth Of*, out of.
205   *that . . . despair*. The sweet seductiveness of despair is noted by
      Spenser. Despair's 'subtle tongue like dropping honey melt'h
      Into the heart', and later the Red Cross Knight succumbs to the
      arguments in favour of suicidal despair. (*Faerie Queene*, I. ix. 31,
      48–51.)

212   *ear*, plough.

AUMERLE: My father hath a power; inquire of him,
  And learn to make a body of a limb.
KING RICHARD: Thou chidest me well. Proud Bolingbroke, I
    come
  To change blows with thee for our day of doom.
  This ague fit of fear is overblown;   190
  An easy task it is to win our own.
  Say, Scroop, where lies our uncle with his power?
  Speak sweetly, man, although thy looks be sour.
SCROOP: Men judge by the complexion of the sky
    The state and inclination of the day;
  So may you by my dull and heavy eye,
    My tongue hath but a heavier tale to say.
  I play the torturer, by small and small
  To lengthen out the worst that must be spoken.
  Your uncle York is joined with Bolingbroke,   200
  And all your northern castles yielded up,
  And all your southern gentlemen in arms
  Upon his party.
KING RICHARD: Thou hast said enough.
  [*To Aumerle*] Beshrew thee cousin, which didst lead me forth
  Of that sweet way I was in to despair.
  What say you now? What comfort have we now?
  By heaven I'll hate him everlastingly
  That bids me be of comfort any more.
  Go to Flint Castle, there I'll pine away.
  A king, woe's slave, shall kingly woe obey.   210
  That power I have, discharge, and let them go
  To ear the land that hath some hope to grow,
  For I have none. Let no man speak again
  To alter this, for counsel is but vain.
AUMERLE: My liege, one word.

215– *He . . . tongue*, i.e. Aumerle's 'My liege', and the possibility of a
16   'false hope'. Flattery was sometimes regarded as poison (*Henry V*,
      IV. i. 232) hence the background suggestion of a double-tongued
      serpent.

    The theme of this scene is virtually that of Sonnet 144, 'Two
loves I have of comfort and despair, Which like two spirits do
suggest (attract) me still'. Its rapid oscillation between high hope
and depths of despair is a well designed prelude to the central
figurative rise and fall in the next scene, and a subtle psychological
device to break down Richard.

Flint Castle

The locality changes during this scene (ll. 49–50, 61, 183) as
occasionally on the Elizabethan stage. See *Julius Cæsar*, III. i. 12,
for a change of scene from the street to the Capitol.

1   *So . . . intelligence*. The device of continued conversation. Should
      Bolingbroke be reading a document? *intelligence*, information.

5–6   *The . . . head*. Northumberland's lack of respect contrasts with his
      flattery of Bolingbroke (II. iii. 2–18).
6   *hid his head*, gone into hiding.
7–9   *It . . . head*. York upholds the divine office of kingship. (See also
      l. 17.) The contrast with Richard's position in the previous scene
      is sharply ironic.

13   *to*, as to.
14   *taking . . . head*, (a) taking such a liberty, (b) omitting his title.
15   *Mistake*, misinterpret.

17   *mistake*, wrongly take. Q, F have no punctuation after 'mistake'
      and the line could be rendered, 'Lest you sin against the heavens
      which are over our heads'.

KING RICHARD: He does me double wrong
  That wounds me with the flatteries of his tongue.
  Discharge my followers, let them hence away,
  From Richard's night to Bolingbroke's fair day.   [*Exeunt*

SCENE THREE

Enter with drum and colours BOLINGBROKE, YORK,
NORTHUMBERLAND *and soldiers*

BOLINGBROKE: So that by this intelligence we learn
  The Welshmen are dispersed, and Salisbury
  Is gone to meet the King, who lately landed
  With some few private friends upon this coast.
NORTHUMBERLAND: The news is very fair and good my lord,
  Richard not far from hence hath hid his head.
YORK: It would beseem the Lord Northumberland
  To say 'King Richard'. Alack the heavy day
  When such a sacred king should hide his head.
NORTHUMBERLAND: Your grace mistakes; only to be brief   10
  Left I his title out.
YORK: The time hath been,
  Would you have been so brief with him, he would
  Have been so brief with you to shorten you,
  For taking so the head, your whole head's length.
BOLINGBROKE: Mistake not, uncle, further than you should.
YORK: Take not, good cousin, further than you should,
  Lest you mistake: the heavens are over our heads.
BOLINGBROKE: I know it uncle, and oppose not myself
  Against their will. But who comes here?

32 *rude ribs*, rough walls.

33 *breath of parley*, trumpet call indicating a wish to talk.

34 *his ruined ears*, its crumbling loopholes. Does the phrase apply also to Richard's state?

40–1 *Provided . . . again*, on condition of the annulment of my banishment and the restoration of my estates.

42 *advantage . . . power*, i.e. the superiority of my army.

45–8 *The . . . show*. After his fearsome threat is this hypocritical or subtle manoeuvring?

48 *stooping duty*, kneeling homage. *tenderly*, solicitously.

Enter PERCY

Welcome Harry. What, will not this castle yield?   20
PERCY: The castle royally is manned my lord,
  Against thy entrance.
BOLINGBROKE: Royally?
  Why it contains no king.
PERCY: Yes, my good lord,
  It doth contain a king. King Richard lies
  Within the limits of yon lime and stone,
  And with him are the Lord Aumerle, Lord Salisbury,
  Sir Stephen Scroop, besides a clergyman
  Of holy reverence, who, I cannot learn.
NORTHUMBERLAND: O belike it is the Bishop of Carlisle.   30
BOLINGBROKE: Noble lord,
  Go to the rude ribs of that ancient castle,
  Through brazen trumpet send the breath of parley
  Into his ruined ears, and thus deliver:
  Henry Bolingbroke
  On both his knees doth kiss King Richard's hand,
  And sends allegiance and true faith of heart
  To his most royal person; hither come
  Even at his feet to lay my arms and power,
  Provided that my banishment repealed   40
  And lands restored again be fully granted;
  If not, I'll use the advantage of my power
  And lay the summer's dust with showers of blood
  Rained from the wounds of slaughtered Englishmen;
  The which, how far off from the mind of Bolingbroke
  It is such crimson tempest should bedrench
  The fresh green lap of fair King Richard's land,
  My stooping duty tenderly shall show.
  Go signify as much while here we march
  Upon the grassy carpet of this plain.   50

51–3 *Let's . . . perused.* Bolingbroke wishes to display the strength of his forces with his peaceable intentions.

52 *tattered,* (a) broken, (b) crenellated.

53 *appointments,* (a) purposes, (b) equipment.

55–7 *elements . . . heaven.* Thunder was supposed to be caused by conflict of lightning and rain. Fire was the superior element, water a lower element.

59 *rain.* Some retain Q's full stop assuming a pun, 'rain', 'reign' (Q 'raigne'), but Bolingbroke had stated that he was 'yielding water', i.e. giving way to the superior element fire. It is possible to take 'yielding' as fruitful, but this seems forced.

62 s.d. F. Trumpeters with Northumberland backstage sound the parley and are answered by other trumpeters in the discovery space. The flourish is perhaps sounded 'within' to herald Richard's appearance on the balcony backstage. Where should Northumberland be and where Bolingbroke during the exchanges between Richard, Northumberland, and Aumerle?

62–7 *See . . . occident.* Is Bolingbroke—awed, moved, excited, admiring, deprecating, contemptuous, jeering? One of Richard's badges was the sun in splendour, a fact Shakespeare probably knew.

63–4 *blushing . . . east.* A red sunrise was proverbially a sign of bad weather and of ill-omen. See *1 Henry IV,* V. i. 1–3.

65 *envious,* hostile.

68–70 *Yet . . . majesty.* Richard's ceremonial appearance rouses York's sympathy and reverence for the royal presence.

68 *Yet,* still.

68–9 *his . . . eagle's.* The analogy with the eagle, the king of birds, conforms to the contemporary view of cosmic order. The eagle was supposed to be able to look at the sun without injury.

69 *lightens forth,* flashes like lightning. See ll. 55–7 note.

72 *We.* The emphatic royal 'we'.

73 *To watch,* waiting for. *fearful,* respectful.

76 *awful,* reverential. *presence,* royal state.

77 *hand,* signature, sign manual. Note the quibble in 'hand', 'handle', ll. 79, 80.

Let's march without the noise of threatening drum,
That from this castle's tattered battlements
Our fair appointments may be well perused.
Methinks King Richard and myself should meet
With no less terror than the elements
Of fire and water when their thundering shock
At meeting tears the cloudy cheeks of heaven.
Be he the fire, I'll be the yielding water;
The rage be his, whilst on the earth I rain
My waters—on the earth, and not on him.   60
March on, and mark King Richard how he looks.

The trumpets sound parley without, and answer within. Then a
flourish. KING RICHARD *appeareth on the walls with the*
BISHOP OF CARLISLE, AUMERLE, SCROOP, *and* SALISBURY

BOLINGBROKE: See, see King Richard doth himself appear,
    As doth the blushing, discontented sun
    From out the fiery portal of the east,
    When he perceives the envious clouds are bent
    To dim his glory, and to stain the track
    Of his bright passage to the occident.
YORK: Yet looks he like a king. Behold his eye,
    As bright as is the eagle's, lightens forth
    Controlling majesty. Alack, alack for woe   70
    That any harm should stain so fair a show!
KING RICHARD: We are amazed, and thus long have we stood
    To watch the fearful bending of thy knee,
    Because we thought ourself thy lawful king.
    And if we be, how dare thy joints forget
    To pay their awful duty to our presence?
    If we be not, show us the hand of God
    That hath dismissed us from our stewardship;
    For well we know no hand of blood and bone
    Can gripe the sacred handle of our sceptre,   80

81   *Unless . . . profane*, without committing sacrilege.

83   *torn their souls*, harmed their souls, sinned. *turning*, forsaking the
      king, committing treason. There is a quibble 'torn', 'turning'
      stressing the sin.

85–8 *Yet . . . unbegot*. A not uncommon notion of the time. See also
      2 Kings, xix. 35; vi. 15–17.

90   *my*. Richard begins to discard his royalty.

93–4 *He . . . war*. Just as the heir to an estate opens the will to confirm
      his inheritance, so Bolingbroke seeks to inherit the kingdom by
      making war the will that bequeaths it to him.

94   *purple*, (a) crimson, blood-stained, (b) ? royal. *testament*, will.
      Possibly the association of the Old and New Testaments (cove-
      nants) with sacrificial blood has influenced the imagery here.

95, 96 *crown, crowns*. Quibble.

97   *flower . . . face*, (a) the beauty of the countryside, (b) the best of
      English youth, (c) human face (with the next two lines).

100   *pastures'*. Some prefer Q, F pastors (pastor's), i.e. Richard.

102   *civil and uncivil*, i.e. civil and barbarous war arranged as a quibble.

106   *grandsire*, Edward III.

108   *head*, spring-head, source.

112   *scope*, aim.

113   *lineal royalties*, hereditary rights due to his royal descent.

Unless he do profane, steal, or usurp.
And though you think that all, as you have done,
Have torn their souls by turning them from us,
And we are barren and bereft of friends,
Yet know, my master God omnipotent,
Is mustering in his clouds on our behalf
Armies of pestilence; and they shall strike
Your children yet unborn and unbegot,
That lift your vassal hands against my head,
And threat the glory of my precious crown.   90
Tell Bolingbroke, for yon methinks he stands,
That every stride he makes upon my land
Is dangerous treason. He is come to open
The purple testament of bleeding war.
But ere the crown he looks for live in peace,
Ten thousand bloody crowns of mothers' sons
Shall ill become the flower of England's face,
Change the complexion of her maid-pale peace
To scarlet indignation, and bedew
Her pastures' grass with faithful English blood.   100
NORTHUMBERLAND: The King of heaven forbid our lord the
    King
Should so with civil and uncivil arms
Be rushed upon. Thy thrice-noble cousin
Harry Bolingbroke doth humbly kiss thy hand;
And by the honourable tomb he swears
That stands upon your royal grandsire's bones,
And by the royalties of both your bloods,
Currents that spring from one most gracious head,
And by the buried hand of warlike Gaunt,
And by the worth and honour of himself,   110
Comprising all that may be sworn or said,
His coming hither hath no further scope
Than for his lineal royalties, and to beg

114   *Enfranchisement*, freedom from banishment and consequent restoration of rights.
115   *on . . . party*, on your majesty's part.
116   *commend*, consign.
117   *barbed*, protected by pieces of leather or armour on chest and flanks.
119–   *This . . . him.* Northumberland does not repeat Bolingbroke's
   20   threat; he stresses Bolingbroke's integrity with a four-fold oath and his own faith in him. Is he sincere or hypocritical?
121   *returns*, replies that.

126   *gentle*, noble. *commends*, greetings.

128   *look so poorly*, appear so servile.

136   *sooth*, flattery, appeasement.
137   *name*, i.e. of king.

140   *Swellest . . . beat.* Any action?
140,   *scope*, (a) permission, (b) opportunity, (c) intent, (d) room.
   141   Is this a bitter echo of 'scope' (l. 112)?
143–6   *What . . . go.* What significance has the change to the third person and the device of hypophora (asking questions and answering them)—detachment, irony, bitterness, indifference, isolation, renunciation, sincere attempt at Christian resignation?

146   *name . . . go.* Richard declares that only God could deprive the king of his office and name. *A*, in.

Enfranchisement immediate on his knees;
Which on thy royal party granted once,
His glittering arms he will commend to rust,
His barbed steeds to stables, and his heart
To faithful service of your majesty.
This swears he as he is a prince and just,
And as I am a gentleman I credit him.   120
KING RICHARD: Northumberland, say thus. The King returns:
His noble cousin is right welcome hither,
And all the number of his fair demands
Shall be accomplished without contradiction.
With all the gracious utterance thou hast
Speak to his gentle hearing kind commends.
[*To Aumerle*] We do debase ourselves, cousin, do we not,
To look so poorly and to speak so fair?
Shall we call back Northumberland and send
Defiance to the traitor, and so die?   130
AUMERLE: No, good my lord. Let's fight with gentle words,
Till time lend friends, and friends their helpful swords.
KING RICHARD: O God, o God, that e'er this tongue of mine,
That laid the sentence of dread banishment
On yon proud man, should take it off again
With words of sooth! O that I were as great
As is my grief, or lesser than my name,
Or that I could forget what I have been,
Or not remember what I must be now!
Swellest thou, proud heart? I'll give thee scope to beat,   140
Since foes have scope to beat both thee and me.
AUMERLE: Northumberland comes back from Bolingbroke.
KING RICHARD: What must the King do now? Must he
    submit?
The King shall do it. Must he be deposed?
The King shall be contented. Must he lose
The name of king? A God's name, let it go.

147   *set of beads*, rosary.

149   *gay apparel*, Richard and his friends were notorious for their extravagance of dress. *almsman's*, of a beggar who received alms.

150   *figured*, decorated.

151   *palmer's*, pilgrim's. A palmer was a pilgrim who wore a palm leaf to show that he had journeyed to Jerusalem.

152   *carved saints*, small wooden carvings of saints.

155   *I'll . . . highway*. Bitter irony. Richard indicates that he will lie low under the highway over which he exercises authority and protection, and furthermore not in hallowed ground.

156   *trade*, (a) traffic, (b) trample (tread, l. 158). A quibble also on tread on one's head, crush, defeat, humiliate.

162   *lodge*, lay, beat down.

164   *play the wantons*, amuse ourselves, make a game of.

165   *pretty match*, ingenious game.

166   *still*, continually.

167   *fretted us*, worn away for us.

168–9   *there . . . eyes*, i.e. a rhyming epitaph. Is this—mocking, naïve, serious, bitter?

170–1   *ill . . . me*. Are the listeners—embarrassed, puzzled, amused, humouring him, unconscious victims of sarcasm?

173–4   *Will . . . die*. Ironically ambiguous. Perhaps also there is a play on 'leave' and 'live'.

175   *You . . . 'Ay'*. Richard mockingly mimics the response to his question indicating that he suspects collusion between Northumberland and Bolingbroke.

176   *base-court*, the outer and lower courtyard mainly used by servants.

I'll give my jewels for a set of beads,
My gorgeous palace for a hermitage,
My gay apparel for an almsman's gown,
My figured goblets for a dish of wood,   150
My sceptre for a palmer's walking-staff,
My subjects for a pair of carved saints,
And my large kingdom for a little grave,
A little, little grave, an obscure grave;
Or I'll be buried in the King's highway,
Some way of common trade, where subjects' feet
May hourly trample on their sovereign's head;
For on my heart they tread now whilst I live;
And buried once, why not upon my head?
Aumerle thou weepest, my tender-hearted cousin.   160
We'll make foul weather with despised tears;
Our sighs and they shall lodge the summer corn,
And make a dearth in this revolting land.
Or shall we play the wantons with our woes,
And make some pretty match with shedding tears?
As thus to drop them still upon one place,
Till they have fretted us a pair of graves
Within the earth, and therein laid—there lies
Two kinsmen digged their graves with weeping eyes.
Would not this ill do well? Well well, I see   170
I talk but idly, and you laugh at me.
Most mighty prince my Lord Northumberland,
What says King Bolingbroke? Will his majesty
Give Richard leave to live till Richard die?
You make a leg, and Bolingbroke says 'Ay'.

NORTHUMBERLAND: My lord, in the base-court he doth attend
To speak with you, may it please you to come down.

178   *glistering Phaethon.* In classical legend the shining one, the son of Apollo, the Sun god, and Clymene, a naiad. He persuaded his father to let him drive the chariot of the sun. Unable to control the horses he came too close to the earth which was saved from burning by a thunderbolt from Zeus which killed Phaethon. His fallen body was taken by naiads into the waters of Eridanus.

     Phaethon's story was intricately emblematized. He was an ambitious prince desirous of self-glory and power; he was a rash boy prince, rejector of counsel and unfit to govern; his ascent was assailed by the Bull, Lion, Scorpion from the Zodiac (factious powerful lords); it was marred by unruly horses (common people); he was stopped by divine intervention and extinguished in his mother's element, water; he was also identified as Lucifer, thrown out of heaven for his rebellious pride. Which of these are relevant? See ll. 55–60.

179   *Wanting the manage*, lacking the horsemanship. *manage*. A technical term for the schooling of horses. *unruly*, rebellious. *jades*, wretched nags.

180–2   *In . . . King.* Quibbles on 'base' and 'court'.

181   *do them grace*, honour them.

183   *night-owls . . . sing*, owls shriek their ill-omens by night when larks should hymn the sun.

184   *What . . . majesty.* Richard descends from the balcony during these speeches through the tiring-house on to the main stage. See note to l. 62.

185   *fondly*, foolishly. *frantic*, mad.

195   *Thus . . . least.* Richard points to his crown.

200–1   *Well . . . get.* Is this—sarcasm, plain-speaking, justification?

203   *want their remedies*, lack the power to cure their causes.

KING RICHARD: Down, down I come like glistering Phaethon,
  Wanting the manage of unruly jades.
  In the base-court? Base-court, where kings grow base   180
  To come at traitors' calls, and do them grace.
  In the base-court come down? Down court, down King,
  For night-owls shriek where mounting larks should sing.
                                        [*Exeunt from above*

BOLINGBROKE: What says his majesty?
NORTHUMBERLAND: Sorrow and grief of heart
  Makes him speak fondly like a frantic man.
  Yet he is come.

              Enter KING RICHARD *attended, below*

BOLINGBROKE: Stand all apart,
  And show fair duty to his majesty.
      [*Kneels*]
  My gracious lord.
KING RICHARD: Fair cousin, you debase your princely knee 190
  To make the base earth proud with kissing it.
  Me rather had my heart might feel your love
  Than my unpleased eye see your courtesy.
  Up cousin, up; your heart is up, I know,
  Thus high at least, although your knee be low.
BOLINGBROKE: My gracious lord, I come but for mine own.
KING RICHARD: Your own is yours, and I am yours and all.
BOLINGBROKE: So far be mine, my most redoubted lord,
  As my true service shall deserve your love.
KING RICHARD: Well you deserve. They well deserve to
      have   200
  That know the strongest and surest way to get.
  Uncle, give me your hands. Nay, dry your eyes;
  Tears show their love, but want their remedies.

204–5 *Cousin . . . heir.* They were both thirty-three years old at this time.

Richard expresses willingness, but makes it plain by using an emphatic proverb that he is acting under duress.

Duke of York's Garden

S.D. *Enter . . . ladies* F; Q 'Enter the Queen with her attendants'.

1 *sport,* pastime.

3 *bowls.* The game was popular and is frequently mentioned by Shakespeare in association with difficulties or diversion from a straight course.

4 *rubs,* obstacles, difficulties. A technical term in bowling.

5 *runs . . . bias.* Bowls are weighted more heavily on one side than on the other, which causes them to run in a curved course. The Queen says that her fortune is not following the true curved course of the bowling but is running awry.

7–8 *can . . . keeps.* Antimetabole or inversion. There is a pun on 'measure', (a) dance, time, (b) amount.

8 *no . . . grief,* cannot limit its grief. Dancing was believed to harmonize discords in the mind.

13 *wanting,* lacking.

14 *remember,* remind.

15 *being altogether had,* since it possesses me wholly.

18 *it boots not,* it is useless.

Cousin, I am too young to be your father,
Though you are old enough to be my heir.
What will you have, I'll give, and willing too;
For do we must what force will have us do.
Set on towards London, cousin, is it so?
BOLINGBROKE: Yea, my good lord.
KING RICHARD: Then I must not say no.

[*Flourish. Exeunt*

SCENE FOUR

Enter the QUEEN *and two* LADIES

QUEEN ISABEL: What sport shall we devise here in this garden
  To drive away the heavy thought of care?
FIRST LADY: Madam we'll play at bowls.
QUEEN ISABEL: 'Twill make me think the world is full of rubs,
  And that my fortune runs against the bias.
SECOND LADY: Madam we'll dance.
QUEEN ISABEL: My legs can keep no measure in delight
  When my poor heart no measure keeps in grief.
  Therefore no dancing, girl. Some other sport.
FIRST LADY: Madam we'll tell tales.   10
QUEEN ISABEL: Of sorrow or of joy?
FIRST LADY: Of either, madam.
QUEEN ISABEL: Of neither, girl.
  For if of joy, being altogether wanting,
  It doth remember me the more of sorrow;
  Or if of grief, being altogether had,
  It adds more sorrow to my want of joy;
  For what I have I need not to repeat,
  And what I want it boots not to complain.

22–3   *And . . . thee*, if my grief were so slight that my weeping could remove it, I would sing for joy and not ask you to weep for me. Singing and music were held to compose and soothe the mind.

    The care that disorders the Queen's mind is not curable by diverting pastimes nor by dancing and music the creators of harmony, paradoxically and symbolically their effect is inverted.

24   s.d. F; Q 'Enter Gardeners'.

26   *My . . . pins*, I will bet my great misery against a trivial row of pins.

28   *Against*, in anticipation of. *forerun*, heralded.

29–39 *Go . . . flowers*. The symbolism of the state as a garden was common and of long pedigree. See Introduction, p. 29.

29   *young* Q; F 'yond' which some prefer. *dangling apricocks*. The words carry apt shades of meaning. Apricot is derived from *praecox*, precocious, upstart, and there was current a false etymology *in aprico coctus*, ripened in the sun, because apricots only grew when turned to the sun. (See J. Minsheu, *The Guide to Tongues*, 1617). This links with Richard's sun image and his favourites. *dangling*, loosely hanging, suggests lack of control and the dependency of hangers-on.

31   *Stoop*, (a) bend (tree branches), (b) bowed (an old man). *prodigal*, (a) abundant, (b) wasteful. *weight*, (a) burden (of sorrow), (b) mass (of fruit).

33–5 *like . . . commonwealth*. The image was well known and has been traced to classical literature. See *Tempest*, I. ii. 80–1.

36   *even*, equal.

37–9 *I . . . flowers*. The parallel of weeds in a garden to persons hostile to the well-being of the state was common. Oddly a poem written about 1462 describes the England of Henry IV as a garden overgrown with weeds. The origin of the comparison may be the parable of the tares in *Matt.*, xiii. 24–30.

40   *compass . . . pale*, small area of an enclosure. *pale*, fence.

42   *firm*, well-controlled.

43   *sea-walled*. See Gaunt's words, II. i. 46–7.

SECOND LADY: Madam I'll sing.
QUEEN ISABEL: 'Tis well that thou hast cause,
   But thou shouldst please me better wouldst thou weep.   20
SECOND LADY: I could weep madam, would it do you good.
QUEEN ISABEL: And I could sing would weeping do me good,
   And never borrow any tear of thee.

Enter GARDENER *and two* SERVANTS

   But stay, here come the gardeners.
   Let's step into the shadow of these trees.
   My wretchedness unto a row of pins
   They'll talk of state; for everyone doth so
   Against a change. Woe is forerun with woe.
                         [*Queen and ladies stand apart*

GARDENER [*to one man*]: Go bind thou up young dangling
   apricocks
   Which like unruly children make their sire   30
   Stoop with oppression of their prodigal weight;
   Give some supportance to the bending twigs.
   Go thou, and like an executioner
   Cut off the heads of too fast-growing sprays,
   That look too lofty in our commonwealth.
   All must be even in our government.
   You thus employed, I will go root away
   The noisome weeds which without profit suck
   The soil's fertility from wholesome flowers.
FIRST MAN: Why should we, in the compass of a pale,   40
   Keep law and form and due proportion,
   Showing as in a model our firm estate,
   When our sea-walled garden, the whole land,
   Is full of weeds, her fairest flowers choked up,
   Her fruit trees all unpruned, her hedges ruined,

46   *knots*, flower-beds designed in intricate patterns.

47   *caterpillars*. See II. iii. 165. The phrase 'caterpillars of the common-wealth' was frequently used for those who exploited others.

48–9 *He . . . leaf*. Perhaps a version of 'whatsoever a man soweth, that shall he also reap' (*Gal.*, vi. 7).

48   *suffered*, allowed. *spring*, initial growth.

49   *fall of leaf*, decay, autumn.

50   *his . . . shelter*. The metaphor suggests the wide ranging authority and protection of the king.

56   *dressed*, cultivated, ordered.

57   *at . . . year*, at the right season.

58   *wound the bark*, i.e. bark-ringing to encourage fruiting. *skin*. With 'blood' in the next line the two notions of tree surgery and blood-letting are mingled.

59   *overproud*, too much swollen. 'Proud', 'blood', 'riches' anticipate the 'great and growing men'.

65   *borne*. A glance at 'bearing' (l. 64). *crown*. Perhaps a quibble on crown of a tree.

68   *Depressed*, brought low, debased.

69   *'Tis doubt*, it is feared.

72   *pressed . . . speaking*. The Queen who has listened in silence likens her anguish to that of prisoners who were pressed to death by weights (*peine forte et dure*) because they refused to speak. The pain of grief which might break the heart was believed to be relieved by speaking. See *Macbeth*, IV. iii. 209–10.

73   *old . . . garden*. See *Genesis*, ii. 15, 'God took the man, and put him into the garden of Eden to dress it'.

Her knots disordered, and her wholesome herbs
Swarming with caterpillars?
GARDENER: Hold thy peace.
  He that hath suffered this disordered spring
  Hath now himself met with the fall of leaf.
  The weeds which his broad-spreading leaves did shelter,   50
  That seemed in eating him to hold him up,
  Are plucked up root and all by Bolingbroke—
  I mean the Earl of Wiltshire, Bushy, Green.
FIRST MAN: What, are they dead?
GARDENER: They are; and Bolingbroke
  Hath seized the wasteful King. O what pity is it
  That he had not so trimmed and dressed his land
  As we this garden. We at time of year
  Do wound the bark, the skin of our fruit trees,
  Lest being overproud in sap and blood,
  With too much riches it confound itself.   60
  Had he done so to great and growing men,
  They might have lived to bear, and he to taste
  Their fruits of duty. Superfluous branches
  We lop away that bearing boughs may live.
  Had he done so, himself had borne the crown,
  Which waste of idle hours hath quite thrown down.
FIRST MAN: What, think you the King shall be deposed?
GARDENER: Depressed he is already, and deposed
  'Tis doubt he will be. Letters came last night
  To a dear friend of the good Duke of York's   70
  That tell black tidings.
QUEEN ISABEL: O I am pressed to death through want of
  speaking.
    [*She comes forward*]
  Thou, old Adam's likeness set to dress this garden,
  How dares thy harsh rude tongue sound this unpleasing news?

75 *suggested*, tempted, prompted.

79 *Divine*, foretell.

82 *breathe*, utter.
83 *hold*, power.
84 *both are weighed*, balanced against each other.

86 *vanities*, (a) vain persons, (b) empty trifles. *light*, (a) of small weight, (b) worthless. For the whole image see *Psalms*, lxii. 9.

89 *odds*, advantage.
90 *Post*, hasten.

93 *Doth . . . me*, is not your message intended for me.

95 *serve me*, deliver it to me.

102 *so that*, if in that way.
105–6 *rue . . . ruth*. Rue, herb of grace, was the emblem of repentance which came by the grace of God. Here it is linked with 'ruth', pity.

  The foreboding of the Queen is given substance by the Gardener. His political allegory of the garden and the state is enlarged by the Queen into a second Fall of man from Eden, the origin of all calamities of the human race, and here for England in particular. The Gardener's image of the balance shows Richard weighed and found wanting, but he has no joy in the thought. The allegory does not advance the action; it sums up the situation, assesses it through the emotions of observers, and predicts the future. It induces sympathy and compassion for Richard (now merely fallen man) but no hatred, only regret.

What Eve, what serpent hath suggested thee
To make a second Fall of cursed man?
Why dost thou say King Richard is deposed?
Darest thou, thou little better thing than earth,
Divine his downfall? Say, where, when, and how
Camest thou by this ill tidings? Speak thou wretch.   80
GARDENER: Pardon me madam, little joy have I
To breathe this news, yet what I say is true.
King Richard he is in the mighty hold
Of Bolingbroke. Their fortunes both are weighed.
In your lord's scale is nothing but himself,
And some few vanities that make him light.
But in the balance of great Bolingbroke
Besides himself are all the English peers,
And with that odds he weighs King Richard down.
Post you to London and you will find it so.   90
I speak no more than everyone doth know.
QUEEN ISABEL: Nimble mischance that art so light of foot,
Doth not thy embassage belong to me,
And am I last that knows it? O thou thinkest
To serve me last that I may longest keep
Thy sorrow in my breast. Come ladies, go
To meet at London London's king in woe.
What, was I born to this that my sad look
Should grace the triumph of great Bolingbroke?
Gardener, for telling me these news of woe,   100
Pray God the plants thou graftest may never grow.
                              [*Exit Queen with her Ladies*
GARDENER: Poor Queen, so that thy state might be no worse,
I would my skill were subject to thy curse.
Here did she fall a tear; here in this place
I'll set a bank of rue, sour herb of grace.
Rue, even for ruth, here shortly shall be seen,
In the remembrance of a weeping queen.   [*Exeunt*

Westminster Hall

S.D.   A ceremonial entry. Consider the positioning in the light of the challenges and of Richard's entry.

4   *wrought . . . King*, either, persuaded Richard to have Gloucester killed, or, collaborated with Richard in contriving Gloucester's death.

5   *office*, action. *timeless*, untimely.

10   *dead*, (a) fatal, (b) past.

12   *restful*. Perhaps because it was free from Gloucester's intrigues.

13   *Calais*. Gloucester was killed there.

14–17 *Amongst . . . England*. Gloucester was killed before Bolingbroke's exile. See I. i. 100. Is Bagot lying, or is Shakespeare assuming that the audience will not notice the discrepancy and seeking to prepare the audience for Aumerle's conspiracy.

17   *Than Bolingbroke's return*, than have Bolingbroke return.

18   *withal*, as well.

ACT FOUR

SCENE ONE

Enter as to Parliament BOLINGBROKE *with the* LORDS AUMERLE,
NORTHUMBERLAND, HARRY PERCY, FITZWATER, SURREY,
the BISHOP OF CARLISLE, *the* ABBOT OF WESTMINSTER,
another LORD, HERALD, *and officers with* BAGOT

BOLINGBROKE: Call forth Bagot.
  Now Bagot, freely speak thy mind
  What thou dost know of noble Gloucester's death,
  Who wrought it with the King, and who performed
  The bloody office of his timeless end.
BAGOT: Then set before my face the Lord Aumerle.
BOLINGBROKE: Cousin, stand forth, and look upon that man.
BAGOT: My Lord Aumerle, I know your daring tongue
  Scorns to unsay what once it hath delivered.
  In that dead time when Gloucester's death was plotted   10
  I heard you say 'Is not my arm of length,
  That reacheth from the restful English court
  As far as Calais to mine uncle's head?'
  Amongst much other talk that very time
  I heard you say that you had rather refuse
  The offer of an hundred thousand crowns
  Than Bolingbroke's return to England,
  Adding withal, how blest this land would be
  In this your cousin's death.
AUMERLE: Princes and noble lords,
  What answer shall I make to this base man?   20

21 *fair stars*, noble birth. Star positions at birth were supposed to influence a person's life. Here, as in *Twelfth Night*, II. v. 127-8, 'stars'=rank, birth.

22 *On equal terms*. Aumerle, of royal blood, would be debased by challenging so inferior a person as Sir John Bagot.

24 *attainder*, accusation.

25 *gage*, glove as pledge. *manual seal*. Usually 'sign manual'. Shakespeare may be quibbling on 'manual', (a) with my own signature, (b) by my own hand.

29 *temper*, (a) noble quality, (b) brightness.

30 *Bagot . . . up*. Why does Bolingbroke forbid Bagot to pick up the gage?

31-2 *Excepting . . . so*. Aumerle angered, seeks to restore his honour, which he considers impugned by his having to challenge Bagot. *Excepting one*, i.e. Bolingbroke. *moved*, enraged.

33 *thy . . . sympathy*. Is this a—sneer, slight, sarcasm, knightly offer? *stand on sympathy*, make a point of, or depend on, compatibility of rank.

34 *in gage*, in pledge.

40 *rapier's*. The actors would be wearing Elizabethan costume and weapons, not those of Richard's period.

45 *appeal*, charge, accusation.

47-8 *to . . . breathing*, to the death.

52-9 *I . . . you*. Not in F. Perhaps the lines were cut in F copy for Surrey addresses Fitzwater by name ignoring 'Another Lord'. The lines weaken the dramatic effect by overdoing the challenges.

52 *I . . . like*, I cast upon the earth a similar pledge.

53 *lies*, accusations of lying.

Shall I so much dishonour my fair stars
On equal terms to give him chastisement?
Either I must, or have mine honour soiled
With the attainder of his slanderous lips.
There is my gage, the manual seal of death,
That marks thee out for hell. I say thou liest,
And will maintain what thou hast said is false
In thy heart-blood, though being all too base
To stain the temper of my knightly sword.

BOLINGBROKE: Bagot, forbear, thou shalt not take it up.　　30

AUMERLE: Excepting one, I would he were the best
In all this presence that hath moved me so.

FITZWATER: If that thy valour stand on sympathy,
There is my gage Aumerle, in gage to thine.
By that fair sun which shows me where thou standest,
I heard thee say, and vauntingly thou spakest it,
That thou wert cause of noble Gloucester's death.
If thou deniest it twenty times, thou liest,
And I will turn thy falsehood to thy heart,
Where it was forged, with my rapier's point.　　40

AUMERLE: Thou darest not, coward, live to see that day.

FITZWATER: Now by my soul, I would it were this hour.

AUMERLE: Fitzwater, thou art damned to hell for this.

PERCY: Aumerle, thou liest, his honour is as true
In this appeal as thou art all unjust;
And that thou art so, there I throw my gage
To prove it on thee to the extremest point
Of mortal breathing. Seize it if thou darest.

AUMERLE: And if I do not, may my hands rot off,
And never brandish more revengeful steel　　50
Over the glittering helmet of my foe.

ANOTHER LORD: I task the earth to the like, forsworn Aumerle,
And spur thee on with full as many lies

54   *hollowed*, shouted.

55   *From . . . sun*, from sunrise to sunset. The time-limit formally prescribed in which single combat could take place. *pawn*, pledge.

56   *Engage it*, accept the challenge.

57   *Who . . . else?* who else . . .? *sets*, (a) makes a wager, challenges, (b) opposes. *throw*, (a) cast (dice), (b) take on the challenge.

62   *in presence*, present.

65   *boy*, (a) not a man, (b) servant. Contemptuous.

66   *lie, lie*, (i) the lie about Aumerle, (ii) so weightily urge.

72   *How . . . horse*, how foolishly do you urge on one already willing. Proverbially, 'Do not spur a free horse'. *fondly*, foolishly. *forward*, willing.

74   *in a wilderness*, i.e. where they could fight without interruption. (See I. i. 64–6.)

76   *There . . . faith*, there is my pledge. Either Fitzwater points to his gage or throws down a second glove.

77   *tie . . . correction*, compel you to undergo severe punishment from me.

78   *this new world*, i.e. Bolingbroke's control of affairs.

83–4   *Some . . . lies.* It is not clear whether Aumerle should pause after 'gage' or 'lies', there are commas after both in Q and F. Perhaps a full stop after 'gage' is preferable.

84   *That*, (a) with which I may prove, (b) to prove that.

    As may be hollowed in thy treacherous ear
    From sun to sun. There is my honour's pawn;
    Engage it to the trial if thou darest.

AUMERLE: Who sets me else? By heaven, I'll throw at all.
    I have a thousand spirits in one breast
    To answer twenty thousand such as you.

SURREY: My Lord Fitzwater, I do remember well   60
    The very time Aumerle and you did talk.

FITZWATER: 'Tis very true, you were in presence then,
    And you can witness with me this is true.

SURREY: As false, by heaven, as heaven itself is true.

FITZWATER: Surrey thou liest.

SURREY: Dishonourable boy,
    That lie shall lie so heavy on my sword
    That it shall render vengeance and revenge
    Till thou, the lie-giver, and that lie do lie
    In earth as quiet as thy father's skull.
    In proof whereof there is my honour's pawn;   70
    Engage it to the trial if thou darest.

FITZWATER: How fondly dost thou spur a forward horse.
    If I dare eat, or drink, or breathe, or live,
    I dare meet Surrey in a wilderness,
    And spit upon him whilst I say he lies,
    And lies, and lies. There is my bond of faith
    To tie thee to my strong correction.
    As I intend to thrive in this new world,
    Aumerle is guilty of my true appeal.
    Besides, I heard the banished Norfolk say   80
    That thou Aumerle didst send two of thy men
    To execute the noble Duke at Calais.

AUMERLE: Some honest Christian trust me with a gage.
    That Norfolk lies, here do I throw down this,

85   *repealed,* recalled from banishment. *to . . . honour,* to put his honour to the trial.

86   *rest under gage,* be suspended under pledge.

89   *signories,* estates.

90   *we.* Bolingbroke assumes the royal 'we' consistent with his actions.

93   *field,* battlefield.

96   *toiled,* exhausted.

99–   *And . . . long.* What dramatic point has this unhistorical restoration
100 of Mowbray's honour?

103–4 *bosom . . . Abraham,* i.e. to heaven. This popular saying comes from the parable of Dives and Lazarus, *Luke,* xvi. 22. Is Bolingbroke hypocritical or sincere?

108   *plume-plucked.* Some see a reference to Æsop's fable of the crow in borrowed feathers who was stripped by the other birds. But 'plumes' were insignia of pride and military honour. See *Troilus and Cressida,* I. iii. 386, 'Ajax employed plucks down Achilles' plumes'; and *Antony and Cleopatra,* III. xii. 3–4.

111   *Ascend . . . descending.* See ll. 181–8; III. iii. 178–83; III. iv. 84–9.

113   *In . . . throne.* Is this blasphemy?

    If he may be repealed to try his honour.
BOLINGBROKE: These differences shall all rest under gage
    Till Norfolk be repealed. Repealed he shall be,
    And though mine enemy, restored again
    To all his lands and signories. When he is returned
    Against Aumerle we will enforce his trial.   90
BISHOP OF CARLISLE: That honourable day shall ne'er be
    seen.
    Many a time hath banished Norfolk fought
    For Jesu Christ in glorious Christian field,
    Streaming the ensign of the Christian cross
    Against black pagans, Turks, and Saracens,
    And toiled with works of war, retired himself
    To Italy, and there at Venice gave
    His body to that pleasant country's earth,
    And his pure soul unto his captain Christ,
    Under whose colours he had fought so long.   100
BOLINGBROKE: Why Bishop, is Norfolk dead?
BISHOP OF CARLISLE: As surely as I live my lord.
BOLINGBROKE: Sweet peace conduct his sweet soul to the
    bosom
    Of good old Abraham. Lords appellants,
    Your differences shall all rest under gage
    Till we assign you to your days of trial.

Enter YORK

YORK: Great Duke of Lancaster I come to thee
    From plume-plucked Richard, who with willing soul
    Adopts thee heir, and his high sceptre yields
    To the possession of thy royal hand.   110
    Ascend his throne, descending now from him,
    And long live Henry, fourth of that name!
BOLINGBROKE: In God's name I'll ascend the regal throne.
BISHOP OF CARLISLE: Marry God forbid.

115– *Worst . . . truth*, though as the meanest in rank in this royal
16 court I speak, yet as a priest I have the greatest obligation to
speak the truth.

119 *noblesse*, nobility.

120 *Learn*, teach.

121– *What . . . king*. This aspect of the Divine Right of Kings, a Tudor
33 political doctrine, occurs in Shakespeare's sources. It appears in
the 'Homily Against Disobedience and Wilful Rebellion', one of
the sermons appointed to be read at intervals in churches.

123 *but*, except when.

124 *apparent*, obvious.

125 *figure*, image.

126 *elect*, chosen.

127 *planted*, established.

128 *breath*, voice.

129 *forfend*, forbid.

130 *climate*, world. *souls refined*, Christian believers.

131 *obscene*, foul.

136– *And . . . woe*. This warning of the evils of rebellion and civil war
49 particularly the deaths of fellow countrymen, of slaughter of each
other by members of the same family, of brother by brother,
father by son, son by father, and the suffering of children and
grandchildren is stressed in the Homily (see note to ll. 121–33)
and appears repeatedly in Shakespeare.

136 *let me prophesy*. Carlisle's prophecy against Bolingbroke balances
Gaunt's against Richard (II. i. 33–68).

137 *manure*, enrich.

139– *Peace . . . skulls*. The reference to the 'place called the place of
44 dead men's skulls' occurs with variations in *Matthew*, *Mark*, and
John. Wells points out that the passage in *John* is included in the
Gospel for Good Friday in the Prayer Book. He might also
have noted that Carlisle's words, 'Peace shall go sleep with
Turks and infidels', echo words from the collect for Good Friday

Worst in this royal presence may I speak,
Yet best beseeming me to speak the truth.
Would God that any in this noble presence
Were enough noble to be upright judge
Of noble Richard. Then true noblesse would
Learn him forbearance from so foul a wrong.   120
What subject can give sentence on his king?
And who sits here that is not Richard's subject?
Thieves are not judged but they are by to hear,
Although apparent guilt be seen in them;
And shall the figure of God's majesty,
His captain, steward, deputy elect,
Anointed, crowned, planted many years,
Be judged by subject and inferior breath,
And he himself not present? O forfend it God,
That in a Christian climate souls refined   130
Should show so heinous, black, obscene a deed!
I speak to subjects, and a subject speaks,
Stirred up by God thus boldly for his king.
My Lord of Herford here, whom you call king,
Is a foul traitor to proud Herford's king;
And if you crown him, let me prophesy
The blood of English shall manure the ground,
And future ages groan for this foul act.
Peace shall go sleep with Turks and infidels,
And in this seat of peace tumultuous wars   140

immediately preceding the gospel extract. The collect is a prayer for bringing all men into 'one fold': 'have mercy upon all Jews, Turks, Infidels, and Heretics, and take from them all ignorance and hardness of heart . . .' (*Book of Common Prayer*, 1552). What dramatic value has this suggestion of Good Friday?

141   *Shall . . . confound*, shall members of one family and one species destroy each other.

145   *raise . . . house*, i.e. the houses of York and Lancaster. Proverbial, see *Mark*, iii. 25; *Matt.*, xii. 25.

154–317   *May . . . fall*. Not in Q. See Introduction, pp. 5–6.

154   *the commons' suit*, i.e. that judgment against Richard should be made public. (See ll. 221–2.)

156   *surrender*, abdicate.

159   *sureties . . . answer*, i.e. friends who will undertake that you will appear to answer your charges at the appointed time.

160–1   *Little . . . hands*. Is Bolingbroke—sarcastic, reproachful, angry, disappointed?

168   *favours*, (a) faces, (b) favours given to.

169–70   *All . . . Christ*. See Introduction, pp. 18, 29, and *Matt.*, xxvi. 49, 'And forthwith when he came to Jesus, he said, Hail master: and kissed him'.

Shall kin with kin, and kind with kind confound.
Disorder, horror, fear, and mutiny
Shall here inhabit, and this land be called
The field of Golgotha and dead men's skulls.
O if you raise this house against this house,
It will the woefullest division prove
That ever fell upon this cursed earth.
Prevent it, resist it, let it not be so,
Lest child, child's children, cry against you woe.

NORTHUMBERLAND: Well have you argued sir, and for your
  pains,   150
  Of capital treason we arrest you here.
  My Lord of Westminster, be it your charge
  To keep him safely till his day of trial.
  May it please you, lords, to grant the commons' suit?

BOLINGBROKE: Fetch hither Richard, that in common view
  He may surrender. So we shall proceed
  Without suspicion.

YORK: I will be his conduct.   [*Exit*

BOLINGBROKE: Lords, you that here are under our arrest,
  Procure your sureties for your days of answer.
  Little are we beholding to your love,   160
  And little looked for at your helping hands.

Enter RICHARD *and* YORK *and officers bearing the regalia*

RICHARD: Alack, why am I sent for to a king
  Before I have shook off the regal thoughts
  Wherewith I reigned? I hardly yet have learned
  To insinuate, flatter, bow, and bend my knee.
  Give sorrow leave awhile to tutor me
  To this submission. Yet I well remember
  The favours of these men. Were they not mine?
  Did they not sometime cry 'All hail!' to me?
  So Judas did to Christ. But he in twelve   170

173   *clerk*. A lay official who leads the responses to prayers and litanies in church services.

175   *And . . . me*, and yet so be it if I am still king in the eyes of heaven.

176   *service*, (a) duty, (b) religious service.

177   *office*, ceremony, religious service. This may carry on the religious overtones.

181   *seize*, (a) formally take possession of, (b) ? take forcibly.

181–2 *Here . . . thine*. How are the two positioned?

183–6 *Now . . . water*. The allegory of Fortune's buckets by which a man's good and bad fortunes were symbolized was well known from medieval times onward. It was the subject of many emblematic woodcuts with interpretive verses.

184   *owes*, has. *filling one another*, i.e. when the full bucket is lifted to the top of the well the empty bucket descends and is filled.

189   *I . . . resign*. Bolingbroke's directness cuts through Richard's emotional self-torture.

190–2 *My . . . those*. Richard emphasizes the distinction between the king's public person and the ordinary man. For a similar linking of grief and majesty see *King John*, III. i. 70–4.

194–6 *Your . . . won*, my grief is due to loss of office that your recent effort has gained.

194   *cares*, (a) anxieties, griefs, (b) responsibilities, offices, (c) troubles, pains.

198   *'tend*, attend upon.
      Does this elaborate quibbling on 'cares' reveal—intense grief, confused mind, reluctance to surrender, indecision, child-like changeability?

Found truth in all but one; I, in twelve thousand, none.
God save the King! Will no man say amen?
Am I both priest and clerk? Well then, amen
God save the King, although I be not he;
And yet amen, if Heaven do think him me.
To do what service am I sent for hither?

YORK: To do that office of thine own good will
Which tired majesty did make thee offer:
The resignation of thy state and crown
To Henry Bolingbroke.

RICHARD: Give me the crown.   180
Here, cousin—seize the crown. Here, cousin—
On this side my hand, and on that side thine.
Now is this golden crown like a deep well
That owes two buckets, filling one another,
The emptier ever dancing in the air,
The other down, unseen, and full of water.
That bucket down, and full of tears am I,
Drinking my griefs, whilst you mount up on high.

BOLINGBROKE: I thought you had been willing to resign.

RICHARD: My crown I am, but still my griefs are mine.   190
You may my glories and my state depose,
But not my griefs; still am I king of those.

BOLINGBROKE: Part of your cares you give me with your
crown.

RICHARD: Your cares set up do not pluck my cares down.
My care is loss of care by old care done;
Your care is gain of care by new care won.
The cares I give, I have, though given away,
They 'tend the crown, yet still with me they stay.

BOLINGBROKE: Are you contented to resign the crown?

200   *Ay . . . ay*, (a) Yes, no; no, yes, (b) I—no, no I, (c) I know no I.
       for . . . be, i.e. if I have lost the name and identity of king. *nothing*,
       (a) nothing, (b) no thing.

201   *Therefore no 'No'*, therefore I cannot say 'no'.

202   *undo*, (a) disrobe, (b) ruin.

203   *heavy weight*, (a) crown, (b) burden of kingly care. Does Richard
       remove the regalia of his office in imagination or in reality?

206–9 *With . . . oaths*. The repetitive structure, anaphora, emphasizes the
       ritual.

206   *balm*, consecrated oil used to anoint him at his coronation.

208   *mine . . . state*, i.e. he betrays his position as God's deputy.

209   *duteous oaths*, oaths of allegiance sworn to me.

215   *with nothing grieved*, (a) not grieved by anything, (b) grieved by
       having nothing.

216   *with all*, (a) with everything, (b) withal, moreover.

221–6 *No . . . deposed*. Holinshed states that there were thirty-three
       articles accusing Richard, and he gives them in detail.

221   *read*, i.e. aloud in public.

224   *state and profit*, government and welfare.

225   *confessing*, your confessing.

227   *ravel out*, unravel, reveal.

228   *weaved-up follies*. Suggestive of the professional fool's motley
       woven from threads of different colours.

231   *read a lecture*, read in public.

232   *heinous article*. The articles of indictment against Richard accused
       him of 'heinous' matters.

RICHARD: Ay, no; no, ay; for I must nothing be.   200
  Therefore no 'No', for I resign to thee.
  Now, mark me how I will undo myself.
  I give this heavy weight from off my head,
  And this unwieldy sceptre from my hand,
  The pride of kingly sway from out my heart.
  With mine own tears I wash away my balm,
  With mine own hands I give away my crown,
  With mine own tongue deny my sacred state,
  With mine own breath release all duteous oaths.
  All pomp and majesty I do forswear;   210
  My manors, rents, revenues I forgo;
  My acts, decrees, and statutes I deny.
  God pardon all oaths that are broke to me;
  God keep all vows unbroke are made to thee.
  Make me, that nothing have, with nothing grieved,
  And thou with all pleased, that hast all achieved.
  Long mayst thou live in Richard's seat to sit,
  And soon lie Richard in an earthy pit.
  God save King Henry, unkinged Richard says,
  And send him many years of sunshine days.   220
  What more remains?
NORTHUMBERLAND: No more, but that you read
  These accusations, and these grievous crimes
  Committed by your person and your followers
  Against the state and profit of this land;
  That by confessing them, the souls of men
  May deem that you are worthily deposed.
RICHARD: Must I do so? And must I ravel out
  My weaved-up follies? Gentle Northumberland,
  If thy offences were upon record,
  Would it not shame thee, in so fair a troop,   230
  To read a lecture of them? If thou wouldst,
  There shouldst thou find one heinous article,

234–5 *And . . . heaven.* The breaking of the oath of allegiance to Richard is stressed in the play; it was seen as a sinful and blasphemous act.

235 *blot,* stain of infamy.

237 *bait,* torment.

238–
41 *Though . . . sin.* See note to III. i. 5–6 and Introduction, pp. 18, 29. The biblical reference is *Matt.,* xxvii. 24–6, where Pilate 'took water, and washed his hands before the people, saying, I am innocent of the blood of this just person . . . and when he had scourged Jesus, he delivered him to be crucified'.

240 *sour,* bitter.

245 *sort,* gang. The loss of 'l' in 'salt' and of 'r' in 'sort' in some Elizabethan pronunciations suggests a play on the two words here (Dobson, *English Pronunciation,* § 398ff).

248–9 *For . . . king.* Another statement of the twofold aspect of a king.

249 *T'undeck . . . king,* to take off the outward trappings of the official figure of a king.

251 *state,* royal position.

253 *haught,* haughty.

254–6 *I . . . usurped.* The importance of the name as the actual thing named is stressed elsewhere: III. ii. 85–7; III. iii. 136–7. Now Richard has lost the name of king he is nothing. The royalty that was his by birth has been usurped and he is a nameless nobody. It may also refer to a story that he was illegitimate and christened John of Bordeaux. The story was available to Shakespeare in Froissart's *Chronicle.*

260 *sun of Bolingbroke.* The sun-image of kingship now belongs to Bolingbroke.

261 *To . . . water-drops.* See III. iii. 54–60 and Introduction, p. 31.

263 *sterling,* valid.

Containing the deposing of a king,
And cracking the strong warrant of an oath,
Marked with a blot, damned in the book of heaven.
Nay, all of you that stand and look upon me,
Whilst that my wretchedness doth bait myself,
Though some of you, with Pilate, wash your hands.
Showing an outward pity—yet you Pilates
Have here delivered me to my sour cross,   240
And water cannot wash away your sin.

NORTHUMBERLAND: My lord dispatch, read o'er these articles.

[Offers a paper

RICHARD: Mine eyes are full of tears, I cannot see.
And yet salt water blinds them not so much
But they can see a sort of traitors here.
Nay, if I turn mine eyes upon myself,
I find myself a traitor with the rest.
For I have given here my soul's consent
T'undeck the pompous body of a king;
Made glory base, and sovereignty a slave;   250
Proud majesty, a subject; state, a peasant.

NORTHUMBERLAND: My lord—

RICHARD: No lord of thine, thou haught insulting man;
Nor no man's lord. I have no name, no title,
No, not that name was given me at the font,
But 'tis usurped. Alack the heavy day,
That I have worn so many winters out,
And know not now what name to call myself.
O that I were a mockery king of snow,
Standing before the sun of Bolingbroke,   260
To melt myself away in water-drops!
Good king, great king, and yet not greatly good,
An if my word be sterling yet in England,
Let it command a mirror hither straight

266   *his*, its.

269   *Fiend . . . hell*. Hysteria, savage contempt, or pretence? *torments* tormentest.

270   *Urge . . . Northumberland*. Is this due to—compassion, tact, confidence in his power?

275   *Give . . . read*. The mirror was the emblem of pride. A wall painting in the church at Hoxne, Suffolk, represented Pride as a richly dressed young man crowned with a sceptre in one hand and a looking-glass in the other. Pride proverbially was succeeded by shame and had a fall (see V. v. 88). It was also the first of the deadly sins, the root of all evil that separated man from God. See *Psalms*, xvi–xviii.

283   *wink*, shut their eyes.

284   *faced*, countenanced.

285   *outfaced*, put out of countenance, superseded.

286–8 *A . . . shivers*. The image of the royal person and the human being is destroyed.

289   *sport*, show.

291–2 *The . . . face*, the outward, superficial expressions of your sorrow have destroyed the mere reflection of your face (authority).

That it may show me what a face I have,
Since it is bankrupt of his majesty.
BOLINGBROKE: Go some of you, and fetch a looking-glass.
                                        [*Exit Attendant*
NORTHUMBERLAND: Read o'er this paper while the glass doth
   come.
RICHARD: Fiend, thou torments me ere I come to hell.
BOLINGBROKE: Urge it no more, my Lord
   Northumberland.   270
NORTHUMBERLAND: The commons will not then be satisfied.
RICHARD: They shall be satisfied. I'll read enough
   When I do see the very book indeed
   Where all my sins are writ, and that's myself.

Enter Attendant with a glass

Give me that glass, and therein will I read.
No deeper wrinkles yet? Hath sorrow struck
So many blows upon this face of mine
And made no deeper wounds? O flattering glass,
Like to my followers in prosperity,
Thou dost beguile me. Was this face the face   280
That every day under his household roof
Did keep ten thousand men? Was this the face
That like the sun did make beholders wink?
Is this the face which faced so many follies,
That was at last outfaced by Bolingbroke?
A brittle glory shineth in this face;
As brittle as the glory is the face,
                            [*He throws the glass down*
For there it is, cracked in an hundred shivers.
Mark, silent King, the moral of this sport,
How soon my sorrow hath destroyed my face.   290
BOLINGBROKE: The shadow of your sorrow hath destroyed
   The shadow of your face.

295   *external . . . laments*, outward shows of grief.

298   *substance*, reality.
298–   *and . . . cause*. Ironic.
  301

301–8 *I . . . beg*. Richard in the exposition of his emotions paradoxically
      dominates this part of the scene. The silence of Bolingbroke is
      sometimes held to be the dominant theme but Richard's per-
      ceptiveness outfaces him.

307   *to*, as.

312   *Then . . . go*. Wells suggests that Richard deflates Bolingbroke by
      the anticlimax of his simple request.

314   *sights*, the view of each of you.

315–   *convey . . . Conveyers*. Richard quibbles on the euphemistic slang
  16   meaning 'steal' and 'thief', and extends it by 'nimbly' where 'nim'
      = thief, or to steal, as well as adroitly, quickly. See *Winter's Tale*,
      IV. iv. 685–6.

320   *pageant*, show, spectacle.

RICHARD: Say that again.
'The shadow of my sorrow'—ha, let's see.
'Tis very true, my grief lies all within,
And these external manners of laments
Are merely shadows to the unseen grief
That swells with silence in the tortured soul.
There lies the substance; and I thank thee King,
For thy great bounty, that not only givest
Me cause to wail, but teachest me the way   300
How to lament the cause. I'll beg one boon,
And then be gone and trouble you no more.
Shall I obtain it?
BOLINGBROKE: Name it, fair cousin.
RICHARD: 'Fair cousin'? I am greater than a king;
For when I was a king my flatterers
Were then but subjects; being now a subject
I have a king here to my flatterer.
Being so great, I have no need to beg.
BOLINGBROKE: Yet ask.
RICHARD: And shall I have?   310
BOLINGBROKE: You shall.
RICHARD: Then give me leave to go.
BOLINGBROKE: Whither?
RICHARD: Whither you will, so I were from your sights.
BOLINGBROKE: Go some of you, convey him to the Tower.
RICHARD: O good, 'convey'? Conveyors are you all,
That rise thus nimbly by a true king's fall.
                          [*Exeunt Richard and Guard*
BOLINGBROKE: On Wednesday next we solemnly set down
Our coronation. Lords, prepare yourselves.
                    [*Exeunt all except the Abbot of Westminster,
                          the Bishop of Carlisle, and Aumerle*
ABBOT OF WESTMINSTER: A woeful pageant have we here
beheld.   320

321–2 *The . . . thorn*. See Introduction, p. 29.

327–8 *take . . . intents*, take the sacrament as a pledge to conceal my plans.
 The scene gathers sympathy for Richard, his emotional agony, his telling thrusts at his enemies, his giving under duress and his taking back, his references to traitors, to Pilate, Judas, and Christ, these together with Carlisle's powerful prophecy make clear the enormity of deposition.

BISHOP OF CARLISLE: The woe's to come; the children yet
    unborn
  Shall feel this day as sharp to them as thorn.
AUMERLE: You holy clergymen, is there no plot
  To rid the realm of this pernicious blot?
ABBOT OF WESTMINSTER: My lord,
  Before I freely speak my mind herein,
  You shall not only take the sacrament
  To bury mine intents, but also to effect
  Whatever I shall happen to devise.
  I see your brows are full of discontent,   330
  Your hearts of sorrow, and your eyes of tears.
  Come home with me to supper, I will lay
  A plot shall show us all a merry day.   [*Exeunt*

2   *Julius . . . tower*. The Tower of London built, according to a belief arising in the Middle Ages, by Julius Cæsar. *ill-erected*, built for shameful purposes, i.e. to imprison Richard.

3   *flint*, (a) flint stone, (b) hard, merciless.

8   *My . . . wither*. Richard was considered the most beautiful of English kings since the Conquest. See *I Henry IV*, I. iii. 175, where Richard is described as 'that sweet, lovely rose'. The rose was not only the emblem of beauty but also of martyrdom.

10   *wash . . . tears*. The true-love, was a four-petalled primrose or an ornament often of four jewels usually pearls. The likeness of pearls to tears was a common image. Hotson, *Mr W.H.*, p. 168 cites Webster, 'I have . . . tears that might be tied in a True-love knot, for they're fresh salt indeed'. Here 'true-love'=(a) sweetheart's, (b) in a true love knot.

11   *the . . . stand*, i.e. Richard is as the ruin of his former self even as the ruins of Troy were when compared with the city in its greatness. *model*, ground plan. *old Troy*. There was a tradition that after the fall of Troy Æneas with his followers came to Britain where his descendant Brut built London naming it Troia nova, or Troynovant.

12   *map*, outline. Richard is the mere outline of his former glorious self.

ACT FIVE

SCENE ONE

Enter the QUEEN *and Ladies*

QUEEN ISABEL: This way the King will come; this is the way
To Julius Cæsar's ill-erected tower,
To whose flint bosom my condemned lord
Is doomed a prisoner by proud Bolingbroke.
Here let us rest, if this rebellious earth
Have any resting for her true King's Queen.

Enter RICHARD *and* GUARD

But soft, but see, or rather do not see,
My fair rose wither. Yet look up, behold,
That you in pity may dissolve to dew,
And wash him fresh again with true-love tears.   10
Ah thou the model where old Troy did stand,
Thou map of honour, thou King Richard's tomb,

13–15 *thou . . . guest.* Richard is the 'beautous inn' where grief is
entertained, Bolingbroke the mere alehouse where triumph
celebrates.

20 *this.* F. Q prints a colon=equivalent to 'namely'. F's full stop
seems preferable as Richard's condition is evident and can be
indicated by a gesture. *sworn brother.* Knights sometimes swore to
share troubles and rewards with each other like brothers. In
I Henry IV Prince Hal states ironically that he is 'sworn brother
to a leash of drawers' (II. iv. 6).

22 *Hie,* hasten.

24–5 *Our . . . down,* by living holy lives we must gain the heavenly
crown that our unhallowed time on earth has cast away.

24 *new world's,* heaven's.

26 *shape,* outward appearance.

29–31 *The . . . o'erpowered.* In the concept of universal order the king
and the lion were each leaders of their order, and comparison of
a king with a lion was common. Rage was natural to a lion, and
as justifiable anger it was evidence of majesty in kings.

32 *correction mildly,* F. Q has the comma after 'correction'. Ure cites
Tyndale: 'If (the child) . . . take the correction meekly, and even
kiss the rod . . .' To 'kiss the rod' a proverbial saying=submit
abjectly.

34 *beasts,* i.e. his rebellious subjects.

37 *sometimes,* former.

42 *betid,* happened.

43 *quite,* requite, cap. F 'quit'.

44 *tale of me.* F has 'fall of me'. Wells cites Sidney's *Astrophel and
Stella* (1591), 'pity the tale of me'.

46 *For why,* because. *senseless,* without feeling. *sympathize,* be moved
by.

And not King Richard; thou most beauteous inn,
Why should hard-favoured grief be lodged in thee,
When triumph is become an alehouse guest?
RICHARD: Join not with grief, fair woman, do not so,
To make my end too sudden. Learn, good soul,
To think our former state a happy dream,
From which awaked, the truth of what we are
Shows us but this. I am sworn brother, sweet,   20
To grim necessity, and he and I
Will keep a league till death. Hie thee to France,
And cloister thee in some religious house.
Our holy lives must win a new world's crown
Which our profane hours here have thrown down.
QUEEN ISABEL: What, is my Richard both in shape and mind
Transformed and weakened? Hath Bolingbroke
Deposed thine intellect? Hath he been in thy heart?
The lion dying thrusteth forth his paw
And wounds the earth, if nothing else, with rage   30
To be o'erpowered; and wilt thou pupil-like
Take the correction mildly, kiss the rod,
And fawn on rage with base humility,
Which art a lion and the king of beasts?
RICHARD: A king of beasts indeed; if aught but beasts
I had been still a happy king of men.
Good sometimes queen, prepare thee hence for France.
Think I am dead, and that even here thou takest,
As from my deathbed, thy last living leave.
In winter's tedious nights sit by the fire   40
With good old folks, and let them tell thee tales
Of woeful ages long ago betid;
And ere thou bid goodnight, to quite their griefs
Tell thou the lamentable tale of me,
And send the hearers weeping to their beds;
For why, the senseless brands will sympathize

47   *heavy accent*, sad tones.

48   *weep . . . out*. For the image see *King John*, IV. i. 106, 'fire is dead with grief'.

49   *some*, i.e. brands.

52   *Pomfret*, Pontefract.

55–9   *thou . . . corruption*. Henry IV (Bolingbroke) quotes Richard's lines (*2 Henry IV*, III. i. 70–7), "Northumberland, thou ladder by the which My cousin Bolingbroke ascends my throne;" . . . "The time shall come," thus did he follow it, "The time will come, that foul sin, gathering heads, Shall break into corruption".

58   *gathering head*, (a) taking up arms in rebellion, (b) swelling like a boil.

59   *corruption*, (a) pus, infected matter, (b) treachery, evil.

61   *helping . . . all*, since you helped him to get all of it.

66   *converts*, changes.

67   *one or both*, i.e. the King, Northumberland, or both.

68   *worthy*, merited.

70   *part*, take leave. *part*, depart.

71–3   *Doubly . . . wife*. Perhaps an echo to the words of the marriage service 'Those whom God hath joined together, let no man put asunder', and, 'to have and to hold . . . till death us do part' (1552).

74–5   *Let . . . made*, i.e. let me say farewell with a kiss that will unmake our marriage vow, yet that cannot be for it was sealed with a kiss.

The heavy accent of thy moving tongue,
And in compassion weep the fire out;
And some will mourn in ashes, some coal-black,
For the deposing of a rightful king.   50

Enter NORTHUMBERLAND

NORTHUMBERLAND: My lord, the mind of Bolingbroke is
   changed.
   You must to Pomfret, not unto the Tower.
   And madam, there is order ta'en for you:
   With all swift speed you must away to France.
RICHARD: Northumberland, thou ladder wherewithal
   The mounting Bolingbroke ascends my throne,
   The time shall not be many hours of age
   More than it is, ere foul sin gathering head
   Shall break into corruption. Thou shalt think,
   Though he divide the realm and give thee half,   60
   It is too little, helping him to all.
   He shall think that thou, which knowest the way
   To plant unrightful kings, wilt know again,
   Being ne'er so little urged, another way
   To pluck him headlong from the usurped throne.
   The love of wicked men converts to fear,
   That fear to hate, and hate turns one or both
   To worthy danger and deserved death.
NORTHUMBERLAND: My guilt be on my head, and there an
   end.
   Take leave and part, for you must part forthwith.   70
RICHARD: Doubly divorced! Bad men, you violate
   A two-fold marriage—'twixt my crown and me,
   And then betwixt me and my married wife.
   Let me unkiss the oath 'twixt thee and me;
   And yet not so, for with a kiss 'twas made.
   Part us, Northumberland; I towards the north,

77   *pines the clime*, afflicts the land.

80   *Hallowmas . . . day.* All Saints' Day, now 1 November, but in Shakespeare's day the Julian calendar was used and this made Hallowmas correspond to 12 November.

84   Sp. H. *Richard.* Q 'King'. F 'North' is plausible. *little policy*, poor statecraft.

88   *near . . . near*, being near, be no nearer meeting. *near*, nearer.

92   *piece . . . out*, lengthen, or eke out the journey.

96   *Thus . . . heart.* The fanciful notion or conceit that lovers exchanged hearts in a kiss was frequent in love poetry.

97–
100   *Give . . . groan*, give me back my heart because it is not good that, having your heart, I should kill it with my grief. (They kiss again.) Now I have my heart again, go, so that I may kill my own heart with my anguish.

101   *We . . . delay*, we are over-indulging our grief with this soft-hearted delay.
      The scene continues to enlist the audience's sympathy for Richard and his Queen. Northumberland's harshness is underlined and his second treachery foretold. The contrast adds to Richard's virtue.

Where shivering cold and sickness pines the clime;
My wife to France, from whence set forth in pomp
She came adorned hither like sweet May,
Sent back like Hallowmas or shortest of day.   80
QUEEN ISABEL: And must we be divided? Must we part?
RICHARD: Ay, hand from hand, my love, and heart from
   heart.
QUEEN ISABEL: Banish us both, and send the King with me.
RICHARD: That were some love, but little policy.
QUEEN ISABEL: Then whither he goes, thither let me go.
RICHARD: So two together weeping make one woe.
  Weep thou for me in France, I for thee here
  Better far off than, near, be ne'er the near.
  Go count thy way with sighs, I mine with groans.
QUEEN ISABEL: So longest way shall have the longest
   moans.   90
RICHARD: Twice for one step I'll groan, the way being short,
  And piece the way out with a heavy heart.
  Come come, in wooing sorrow let's be brief,
  Since wedding it, there is such length in grief.
  One kiss shall stop our mouths, and dumbly part;
  Thus give I mine, and thus take I thy heart.

                               [They kiss

QUEEN ISABEL: Give me mine own again; 'twere no good
   part
  To take on me to keep and kill thy heart.

                               [They kiss

  So, now I have mine own again, be gone,
  That I may strive to kill it with a groan.   100
RICHARD: We make woe wanton with this fond delay.
  Once more adieu, the rest let sorrow say.   *[Exeunt*

Duke of York's house

2   *When . . . off.* See V. i. 44–5.
3   *cousins,* i.e. Richard and Bolingbroke.

5–6   *Where . . . head.* The description is repeated in *2 Henry IV*, I. iii. 103–7.
5   *windows' tops,* topmost windows.

8–9   *hot . . . know.* The horse was Richard's roan Barbary. It seemed by its fiery behaviour to be aware of Bolingbroke's high ambitions. The element fire naturally aspired to the highest position.

13   *greedy looks,* i.e. they devoured him with their eyes.

15–16 *walls . . . said,* you would have thought from the multitude of eager faces peering from the windows that the walls were hung with painted cloths which cried out all together. Painted cloths were hung in the streets during a pageant or ceremonial procession. Figures on the cloths sometimes had words depicted as coming from their mouths.
19   *lower,* i.e. bowing lower.
21   *still,* continually.

24   *well graced,* accomplished or applauded.
25   *idly,* without interest.

SCENE TWO

Enter DUKE OF YORK *and the* DUCHESS

DUCHESS OF YORK: My lord, you told me you would tell the rest,
  When weeping made you break the story off,
  Of our two cousins' coming into London.
YORK: Where did I leave?
DUCHESS OF YORK: At that sad stop, my lord,
  Where rude misgoverned hands from windows' tops
  Threw dust and rubbish on King Richard's head.
YORK: Then, as I said, the Duke, great Bolingbroke,
  Mounted upon a hot and fiery steed
  Which his aspiring rider seemed to know,
  With slow but stately pace kept on his course,   10
  Whilst all tongues cried 'God save thee, Bolingbroke'
  You would have thought the very windows spake,
  So many greedy looks of young and old
  Through casements darted their desiring eyes
  Upon his visage, and that all the walls
  With painted imagery had said at once
  'Jesu preserve thee, welcome Bolingbroke'.
  Whilst he from the one side to the other turning,
  Bare-headed, lower than his proud steed's neck,
  Bespake them thus, 'I thank you countrymen'.   20
  And thus still doing, thus he passed along.
DUCHESS OF YORK: Alack poor Richard, where rode he the whilst?
YORK: As in a theatre the eyes of men,
  After a well-graced actor leaves the stage,
  Are idly bent on him that enters next,
  Thinking his prattle to be tedious;
  Even so, or with much more contempt, men's eyes

28   *gentle*, noble . Not in F.

32–3 *tears . . . patience*. A frequent image. See *Twelfth Night*, II. iv. 114–15, for patience in grief.

33   *badges*, outward signs.

38   *bound . . . contents*, in duty bound accept with peaceful contentment.

41   *Aumerle that was*. Aumerle was deprived of his dukedom by the new parliament because in the last parliament he had been an appellant against the Duke of Gloucester. See IV. i. 8–13.

46–7 *who . . . spring*, who are the new favourites in the new court?

50   *bear you well*, behave discreetly.

51   *cropped*, beheaded.

52   *What . . . hold?* According to Holinshed the Abbot of Westminster arranged for a tournament at Oxford during which Bolingbroke was to be murdered and Richard restored to the throne. Aumerle was one of the plotters.

56   *seal*. The red wax seal impressed on a strip of parchment and hanging from the bottom of the document. *without*, outside.

Did scowl on gentle Richard. No man cried 'God save him'.
No joyful tongue gave him his welcome home;
But dust was thrown upon his sacred head,   30
Which with such gentle sorrow he shook off,
His face still combating with tears and smiles,
The badges of his grief and patience,
That had not God for some strong purpose steeled
The hearts of men, they must perforce have melted,
And barbarism itself have pitied him.
But heaven hath a hand in these events,
To whose high will we bound our calm contents.
To Bolingbroke are we sworn subjects now,
Whose state and honour I for aye allow.   40

Enter AUMERLE

DUCHESS OF YORK: Here comes my son Aumerle.
YORK: Aumerle that was,
  But that is lost for being Richard's friend;
  And madam, you must call him Rutland now.
  I am in Parliament pledge for his truth
  And lasting fealty to the new-made King.
DUCHESS OF YORK: Welcome, my son, who are the violets
    now
  That strew the green lap of the new-come spring?
AUMERLE: Madam, I know not, nor I greatly care not.
  God knows I had as lief be none as one.
YORK: Well, bear you well in this new spring of time,   50
  Lest you be cropped before you come to prime.
  What news from Oxford? Do these justs and triumphs hold?
AUMERLE: For aught I know, my lord, they do.
YORK: You will be there, I know.
AUMERLE: If God prevent not, I purpose so.
YORK: What seal is that that hangs without thy bosom?
  Yea, lookest thou pale? Let me see the writing.

65–8   *'Tis . . . to?* The Duchess suggests that Aumerle has raised a loan to buy clothes, and that the document is a pledge to repay the loan. York dismisses this curtly saying that if it were so, the creditor, not Aumerle, would hold the bond.

65   *bond . . . into,* debt that he has incurred. *entered into,* engaged himself, pledged.

79   *appeach,* inform against, impeach.

AUMERLE: My lord, 'tis nothing.

YORK: No matter then who see it.
I will be satisfied, let me see the writing.

AUMERLE: I do beseech your grace to pardon me.   60
It is a matter of small consequence,
Which for some reasons I would not have seen.

YORK: Which for some reasons sir, I mean to see
I fear, I fear—

DUCHESS OF YORK: What should you fear?
'Tis nothing but some bond that he is entered into
For gay apparel 'gainst the triumph day.

YORK: Bound to himself? What doth he with a bond
That he is bound to? Wife, thou art a fool.
Boy, let me see the writing.

AUMERLE: I do beseech you pardon me, I may not show it. 70

YORK: I will be satisfied, let me see it I say.

                    [*He plucks it out of his bosom, and reads it*

YORK: Treason, foul treason! Villain, traitor, slave!

DUCHESS OF YORK: What is the matter my lord?

YORK: Ho, who is within there? Saddle my horse.
God for his mercy, what treachery is here!

DUCHESS OF YORK: Why what is it my lord?

YORK: Give me my boots I say. Saddle my horse.
Now by mine honour, by my life, by my troth,
I will appeach the villain.

DUCHESS OF YORK: What is the matter?

YORK: Peace foolish woman. 80

DUCHESS OF YORK: I will not peace. What is the matter
Aumerle?

AUMERLE: Good mother be content, it is no more
Than my poor life must answer.

DUCHESS OF YORK: Thy life answer?

YORK: Bring me my boots. I will unto the King.

85   *Strike . . . amazed.* The Duchess urges Aumerle to strike the servant in order to hinder York's departure, but Aumerle is too bemused to do so.

90   *Have . . . sons?* Shakespeare disregards York's other son Richard, and that Aumerle was the son of York's first wife.

91   *teeming date*, child-bearing period.

95   *fond*, foolish.

98   *interchangeably . . . hands.* The document was torn into the same number of pieces as the signees, each part was signed by all of them and then sealed.

99   *He . . . none*, he shall not be one of them.

100   *that*, i.e. the conspiracy.

102   *groaned*, i.e. in childbirth.

Act Five, Scene Two

Enter servant with his boots

DUCHESS OF YORK: Strike him Aumerle. Poor boy thou art
    amazed.
    [*To servant*] Hence, villain, never more come in my sight.
YORK: Give me my boots I say.
DUCHESS OF YORK: Why York what wilt thou do?
    Wilt thou not hide the trespass of thine own?
    Have we more sons? Or are we like to have?   90
    Is not my teeming date drunk up with time?
    And wilt thou pluck my fair son from mine age,
    And rob me of a happy mother's name?
    Is he not like thee? Is he not thine own?
YORK: Thou fond mad woman,
    Wilt thou conceal this dark conspiracy?
    A dozen of them here have ta'en the sacrament
    And interchangeably set down their hands
    To kill the King at Oxford.
DUCHESS OF YORK: He shall be none;
    We'll keep him here, then what is that to him?   100
YORK: Away fond woman, were he twenty times my son
    I would appeach him.
DUCHESS OF YORK: Hadst thou groaned for him
    As I have done, thou wouldst be more pitiful.
    But now I know thy mind, thou dost suspect
    That I have been disloyal to thy bed,
    And that he is a bastard, not thy son.
    Sweet York, sweet husband, be not of that mind.
    He is as like thee as a man may be,
    Not like to me, or any of my kin,   109
    And yet I love him.
YORK: Make way unruly woman.   [*Exit*
DUCHESS OF YORK: After, Aumerle. Mount thee upon his
    horse,

112   *Spur post*, ride hard.

The scene depicts both the grandeur and popularity of Boling-broke, and how the patient endurance and maltreatment of Richard moves to tears those who know him. York accepts the situation as due to the inscrutable will of God, but his loyalty is tested immediately by the discovery of Aumerle's conspiracy and for once he acts with resolution. Is the situation—ironic, absurd, pathetic, tragic, subtly prophetic (father against son), reminiscent of Gaunt's decision (I. iii. 236–46)?

Windsor Castle

1   *Can . . . son?* Is this forward-looking to *1* and *2 Henry IV* and *Henry V*, or a sympathetic linkage with York and Aumerle in the last scene? Legends of Prince Hal's profligate youth were common and of long-standing. He was historically only twelve years old at this time. *unthrifty*, prodigal, dissolute.

3   *plague . . . us*, affliction or disaster threaten me. See III. iii. 85–90; IV. i. 137–47.

9   *watch*, watchmen. *passengers*, passers by.

10   *While*. Q, F 'Which'. *wanton*, undisciplined youth.

11   *on*, as.

15   *gallant*. Ironical.

16   *stews*, brothels.

17–19 *And . . . challenger*. In a tournament a knight sometimes wore a token from a lady. By defeating all challengers he would maintain that his lady was the fairest and most virtuous present.

Spur post, and get before him to the King,
And beg thy pardon ere he do accuse thee.
I'll not be long behind—though I be old,
I doubt not but to ride as fast as York;
And never will I rise up from the ground
Till Bolingbroke have pardoned thee. Away, be gone.

[Exeunt

SCENE THREE

Enter BOLINGBROKE *now* KING HENRY, PERCY, *and other lords*

KING HENRY: Can no man tell me of my unthrifty son?
  'Tis full three months since I did see him last.
  If any plague hang over us, 'tis he.
  I would to God, my lords, he might be found.
  Inquire at London 'mongst the taverns there,
  For there, they say, he daily doth frequent
  With unrestrained loose companions,
  Even such, they say, as stand in narrow lanes
  And beat our watch, and rob our passengers,
  While he, young wanton, and effeminate boy,   10
  Takes on the point of honour to support
  So dissolute a crew.
PERCY: My lord, some two days since I saw the Prince,
  And told him of those triumphs held at Oxford.
KING HENRY: And what said the gallant?
PERCY: His answer was, he would unto the stews,
  And from the commonest creature pluck a glove,
  And wear it as a favour, and with that
  He would unhorse the lustiest challenger.
KING HENRY: As dissolute as desperate. Yet through both 20

23   s.D. *amazed*, distraught, agitated.

30   *My . . . mouth*. Perhaps an echo of *Psalms*, cxxxvii. 6, 'let my tongue cleave to the roof of my mouth'.

33   *on the first*, i.e. intended. *first*, former.
34   *after-love*, future loyalty.

40   *safe*, harmless. What action is required?

42   *secure*, over-confident.
43   *Shall . . . face*, must I out of loyalty to you speak treason—by calling you foolhardy—to your face.

I see some sparks of better hope, which elder years
May happily bring forth. But who comes here?

Enter AUMERLE *amazed*

AUMERLE: Where is the King?
KING HENRY: What means our cousin, that he stares and
  looks so wildly?
AUMERLE: God save your grace. I do beseech your majesty
  To have some conference with your grace alone.
KING HENRY: Withdraw yourselves, and leave us here alone.
                         [Exeunt Percy and lords
  What is the matter with our cousin now?
AUMERLE: For ever may my knees grow to the earth,
  My tongue cleave to my roof within my mouth,   30
  Unless a pardon ere I rise or speak.
KING HENRY: Intended or committed was this fault?
  If on the first, how heinous e'er it be,
  To win thy after-love I pardon thee.
AUMERLE: Then give me leave that I may turn the key,
  That no man enter till my tale be done.
KING HENRY: Have thy desire.
            [The Duke of York knocks at the door and crieth
YORK [*within*]: My liege beware, look to thyself,
  Thou hast a traitor in thy presence there.
KING HENRY: Villain, I'll make thee safe   40
                       [Draws his sword
AUMERLE: Stay thy revengeful hand, thou hast no cause to fear.
YORK: Open the door, secure foolhardy King.
  Shall I for love speak treason to thy face?
  Open the door, or I will break it open.

King Henry opens the door. Enter YORK

KING HENRY: What is the matter uncle? Speak, recover
  breath,

49   *my . . . show*, i.e. through lack of breath.
50   *passed*, made.

52   *hand*, what my hand wrote.

55   *Fear . . . penitence*, i.e. attrition not contrition and therefore not genuine.
57   *A . . . heart*. See III. ii. 131.

60   *sheer*, pure.

63   *converts*, changes (in Aumerle).

65   *digressing*, transgressing, straying.
66   *virtue . . . bawd*, serve as pander to his vice. Paradox. See *Romeo and Juliet*, II. iii. 21, 'Virtue itself turns vice being misapplied', and *Hamlet*, III. iv. 154.
67   *spend*, waste.
69   *when . . . dies*, i.e. when Aumerle is executed.

Tell us how near is danger,
That we may arm us to encounter it.
YORK: Peruse this writing here, and thou shalt know
The treason that my haste forbids me show.
AUMERLE: Remember, as thou readest, thy promise passed. 50
I do repent me, read not my name there,
My heart is not confederate with my hand.
YORK: It was, villain, ere thy hand did set it down.
I tore it from the traitor's bosom, King.
Fear, and not love, begets his penitence.
Forget to pity him lest thy pity prove
A serpent that will sting thee to the heart.
KING HENRY: O heinous, strong, and bold conspiracy!
O loyal father of a treacherous son!
Thou sheer, immaculate and silver fountain   60
From whence this stream through muddy passages
Hath held his current and defiled himself.
Thy overflow of good converts to bad,
And thy abundant goodness shall excuse
This deadly blot in thy digressing son.
YORK: So shall my virtue be his vice's bawd,
An he shall spend mine honour with his shame,
As thriftless sons their scraping fathers' gold.
Mine honour lives when his dishonour dies,
Or my shamed life in his dishonour lies.   70
Thou killest me in his life—giving him breath,
The traitor lives, the true man's put to death.
DUCHESS OF YORK [*within*]: What ho, my liege, for God's
sake let me in.
KING HENRY: What shrill-voiced suppliant makes this eager
cry?
DUCHESS OF YORK: A woman, and thy aunt, great King—
'tis I.

78–9   *Our . . . King*. Bolingbroke at least has a sense of humour.
79   '*The . . . King*'. Probably a reference to a popular ballad about
       King Cophetua and the beggar maid which according to Marston
       was 'some roguy thing' and not the pleasant ballad printed in
       Percy's *Reliques*. See *Love's Labour's Lost* (Arden edn.), I. ii. 103–4;
       IV. i. 66, 67 and note.

84–5   *This . . . confound*, if this diseased limb (Aumerle) is cut off the
       others will remain healthy; but if it is left untouched it will infect
       and destroy all the others.

87   *Love . . . can*, if York does not love himself in his own son, he is
       incapable of loving any one else, e.g. Bolingbroke.
88   *make*, do.
89   *Shall . . . rear*, are you, now too old to suckle a child, going to
       rear again this traitor.

92   *walk . . . knees*. A customary form of penance.

96   *Unto*, at one with.

97   *true*, loyal.

102   *would be denied*, inwardly wishes to be refused.

Speak with me, pity me, open the door,
A beggar begs that never begged before.
KING HENRY: Our scene is altered from a serious thing,
And now changed to 'The Beggar and the King'.
My dangerous cousin, let your mother in,   80
I know she is come to pray for your foul sin.

Enter DUCHESS

YORK: If thou do pardon, whosoever pray,
More sins for this forgiveness prosper may.
This festered joint cut off, the rest rest sound;
This let alone will all the rest confound.
DUCHESS OF YORK: O King, believe not this hard-hearted man.
Love loving not itself, none other can.
YORK: Thou frantic woman, what dost thou make here?
Shall thy old dugs once more a traitor rear?
DUCHESS OF YORK: Sweet York be patient. Hear me
    gentle liege.   [*Kneels* 90
KING HENRY: Rise up good aunt.
DUCHESS OF YORK: Not yet, I thee beseech.
For ever will I walk upon my knees,
And never see day that the happy sees
Till thou give joy, until thou bid me joy
By pardoning Rutland my transgressing boy.
AUMERLE: Unto my mother's prayers I bend my knee.
                                              [*He kneels*
YORK: Against them both my true joints bended be.
                                              [*He kneels*
Ill mayst thou thrive if thou grant any grace.
DUCHESS OF YORK: Pleads he in earnest? Look upon his face.
His eyes do drop no tears, his prayers are in jest,   100
His words come from his mouth, ours from our breast.
He prays but faintly, and would be denied,

105   *still*, for ever.

118   *Pardonne-moi*, i.e. a polite refusal of a request.

121   *sets . . . word*, makes the word oppose itself.

123   *chopping*, changing (of meaning), i.e. by frenchifying.
124   *to . . . there*, to show pity, let your tongue utter it.
125   *in . . . ear*, give your heart the sensibility to pity. *piteous*, capable
      of pity.
127   *rehearse*, speak. A rhyme with 'pierce'.

129   *suit . . . hand*, (a) colour of my cards, (b) request I am making.

131   *happy vantage*, (a) blessed posture, (b) fortunate benefit.

We pray with heart and soul, and all beside.
His weary joints would gladly rise I know,
Our knees still kneel till to the ground they grow.
His prayers are full of false hypocrisy,
Ours of true zeal and deep integrity.
Our prayers do outpray his—then let them have
That mercy which true prayer ought to have.

KING HENRY: Good aunt stand up.
DUCHESS OF YORK: Nay, do not say 'Stand up'. 110
Say 'Pardon' first, and afterwards, 'Stand up'.
An if I were thy nurse thy tongue to teach,
'Pardon' should be the first word of thy speech.
I never longed to hear a word till now.
Say 'Pardon', King, let pity teach thee how.
The word is short, but not so short as sweet.
No word like 'Pardon' for kings' mouths so meet.

YORK: Speak it in French, King, say 'Pardonne-moi'.
DUCHESS OF YORK: Dost thou teach pardon pardon to
    destroy?
Ah, my sour husband, my hard-hearted lord,   120
That sets the word itself against the word.
Speak 'Pardon' as 'tis current in our land,
The chopping French we do not understand.
Thine eye begins to speak, set thy tongue there;
Or in thy piteous heart plant thou thine ear,
That hearing how our plaints and prayers do pierce,
Pity may move thee 'Pardon' to rehearse.

KING HENRY: Good aunt stand up.
DUCHESS OF YORK: I do not sue to stand.
Pardon is all the suit I have in hand.

KING HENRY: I pardon him, as God shall pardon me.   130
DUCHESS OF YORK: O happy vantage of a kneeling knee,
    Yet am I sick for fear. Speak it again.

133   *Twice . . . twain.* Possibly saying pardon twice does not pardon someone else (? another conspirator). 'Twain' may be a variant form of 'to twin' = to divide.

135   *god on earth.* A common view of a king. Here the exercise of mercy as a godlike attribute parallels Portia's speech, *Merchant of Venice*, IV. i. 189–98.

136   *brother-in-law.* John Holland, Duke of Exeter, Richard's half-brother by his mother's first husband and husband of Bolingbroke's sister Elizabeth. *abbot,* of Westminster (IV. i.).

137   *consorted,* associated.

139   *powers,* forces.

145   *old . . . new.* As in baptism the old Adam is buried (i.e. sins are forgiven) and the child is made new (*Book of Common Prayer*, Baptismal Service, and *2 Cor.*, v. 17).

S.D.   Q has 'Manet Sir Pierce Exton, etc', but after Bolingbroke's command, 'Withdraw yourselves, and leave us here alone' (V. iii. 27) he cannot have remained on stage.

5   *urged it,* repeated it, insisted on it.

7   *wishtly,* intently, longingly. Perhaps a variant form of 'wistly'.

11   *rid,* get rid of.

Twice saying 'Pardon' doth not pardon twain,
But makes one pardon strong.
KING HENRY: With all my heart
I pardon him.
DUCHESS OF YORK: A god on earth thou art.
KING HENRY: But for our trusty brother-in-law and the
     abbot,
With all the rest of that consorted crew,
Destruction straight shall dog them at the heels.
Good uncle, help to order several powers
To Oxford, or where'er these traitors are.   140
They shall not live within this world, I swear,
But I will have them if I once know where.
Uncle farewell, and cousin adieu.
Your mother well hath prayed, and prove you true.
DUCHESS OF YORK: Come my old son, I pray God make
     thee new.   [*Exeunt*

SCENE FOUR

Enter SIR PIERS EXTON *and* SERVANT

EXTON: Didst thou not mark the King what words he spake?
'Have I no friend will rid me of this living fear?'
  Was it not so?
SERVANT: These were his very words.
EXTON: 'Have I no friend?' quoth he. He spake it twice,
  And urged it twice together, did he not?
SERVANT: He did.
EXTON: And speaking it, he wishtly looked on me,
  As who should say 'I would thou wert the man
  That would divorce this terror from my heart'—
  Meaning the King at Pomfret. Come let's go.   10
  I am the King's friend, and will rid his foe.   [*Exeunt*

A prison in Pomfret Castle

1–66 This is the only soliloquy in the play. Is its function—to give information, advance the action, comment on the situation, comment on any theme in the play, reveal Richard's reactions and his attitude of mind?

5 *hammer it out*, work it out. Perhaps an earlier version of the 'forgetive' action of the brain (*2 Henry IV*, IV. iii. 107).

8 *generation*, offspring. *still-breeding*, ever producing.

9 *this little world*, (a) prison, (b) his own body.

10 *humours*, temperaments. *this world*, i.e. this real world.

13 *scruples*, doubts.

13–14 *set . . . word*, quote one passage of scripture as disagreeing with another. See V. iii. 121.

15–17 *Come . . . eye*. Both passages occur in the same chapter in each of the synoptic gospels: *Matt.*, xix. 14, 24; *Mark*, x. 14, 25; *Luke*, xviii. 16, 25: 'Suffer little children to come unto me and forbid them not: for unto such belongeth the kingdom of God'. 'For it is easier for a camel to go through a needle's eye, than for a rich man to enter into the kingdom of God'. Shakespeare apparently combines the available differing interpretations of this second reference: 'camel', (a) cable-rope, (b) animal. It is the contrast between the welcome to little children and the obstacles in the way of the rich young ruler that Richard considers.

17 *postern*, small gate in a city wall. *needle*. Pronounced as one syllable 'neeld' or 'neel'. See *Midsummer Night's Dream*, III. ii. 204.

19–21 *how . . . walls*. Proverbially hunger tears down stone walls. The proverb may echo one of Holinshed's suggestions that Richard died of starvation.

20 *ribs*, frame.

21 *ragged*, rough, rugged.

25 *silly*, simple.

SCENE FIVE

Enter RICHARD *alone*

RICHARD: I have been studying how I may compare
This prison where I live unto the world;
And for because the world is populous,
And here is not a creature but myself,
I cannot do it. Yet I'll hammer it out.
My brain I'll prove the female to my soul,
My soul the father, and these two beget
A generation of still-breeding thoughts,
And these same thoughts people this little world,
In humours like the people of this world.   10
For no thought is contented. The better sort,
As thoughts of things divine, are intermixed
With scruples, and do set the word itself
Against the word,
As thus: 'Come, little ones'; and then again,
'It is as hard to come as for a camel
To thread the postern of a small needle's eye'.
Thoughts tending to ambition, they do plot
Unlikely wonders: how these vain weak nails
May tear a passage through the flinty ribs   20
Of this hard world, my ragged prison walls;
And for they cannot, die in their own pride.
Thoughts tending to content flatter themselves
That they are not the first of fortune's slaves,
Nor shall not be the last; like silly beggars,

26–7   *refuge . . . That*, console their feeling of shame by thinking that.

33   *treasons*, i.e. the thought of treasons against me.

40–1   *With . . . nothing*, shall be pleased by anything—or, by having nothing—until relieved by death he becomes nothing. The internal rhyme helps to mark the antimetabole and stress the epigrammatic quality.

42   *Ha, ha.* Exclamations of irritation at the lack of time.

43   *When . . . kept*, when the rhythm breaks down and harmonies are not maintained.

46   *check*, reprove. *disordered string*, a string out of place. *string*, stringed instrument.

47–8   *But . . . broke*, but as regards the harmony of my own kingdom and rule, I did not sense that the rightful order had broken down.

49   *waste*, (a) ruin, (b) waste away. Another epigrammatic antimetabole.

50   *numbering clock*, i.e. with moving hands and a dial, not a sundial or an hour-glass.

51–4   *My . . . tears*, my sad thoughts are like minutes and the sighs they give out measure like the ticking of a clock the intervals of wakefulness on my eyes where tears wiped by my fingers are the dial points continuously wiped by the clock hands.

51   *jar*, (a) tick, (b) jerk forward.

52   *watches*, (a) intervals of time, (b) periods of wakefulness.

58   *times*, whole periods.

58–9   *But . . . joy*, but my time now wastes quickly away while Bolingbroke rules in joy.

Who sitting in the stocks refuge their shame,
That many have, and others must sit there;
And in this thought they find a kind of ease,
Bearing their own misfortunes on the back
Of such as have before endured the like.   30
Thus play I in one person many people,
And none contented. Sometimes am I king,
Then treasons make me wish myself a beggar,
And so I am. Then crushing penury
Persuades me I was better when a king,
Then am I kinged again; and by and by
Think that I am unkinged by Bolingbroke,
And straight am nothing. But whate'er I be,
Nor I, nor any man that but man is,
With nothing shall be pleased, till he be eased   40
With being nothing. Music do I hear.   [*The music plays*
Ha, ha; keep time! How sour sweet music is
When time is broke, and no proportion kept.
So is it in the music of men's lives.
And here have I the daintiness of ear
To check time broke in a disordered string,
But for the concord of my state and time,
Had not an ear to hear my true time broke.
I wasted time, and now doth time waste me;
For now hath time made me his numbering clock;   50
My thoughts are minutes, and with sighs they jar
Their watches on unto mine eyes, the outward watch
Whereto my finger like a dial's point,
Is pointing still, in cleansing them from tears.
Now sir, the sound that tells what hour it is
Are clamorous groans which strike upon my heart,
Which is the bell; so sighs, and tears, and groans
Show minutes, times, and hours. But my time

59   *posting*, hastening.

60   *jack . . . clock*. The small mechanical man who strikes the divisions of time on some clocks.

62   *though . . . wits*. Music was supposed to calm the savage breast and to restore sanity. See *King Lear*, IV. vii. 25ff.

66   *strange brooch*, rare jewel.
        Richard's personifications range from ambition to contentment, the king to the beggar, both prisoners. The music with its broken time recalls his past waste of time and breach of harmonious rule, it reflects his present grief which measures merely the period of Bolingbroke's triumph, and perhaps it is ominously foreboding.

67–8   *noble . . . dear*, the cheapest present (myself) and your equal is ten groats too dear. The jest is upon 'royal' or 'rial' which was ten groats more than the coin 'noble'.

67   *peer*, (a) lord, (b) equal.

70   *sad dog*, dismal wretch.

71   *make misfortune live*, prolong my unfortunate life.

75   *sometimes*, former.

76   *earned*, grieved.

78   *Barbary*. The name of Richard's horse, also the name of a highly esteemed breed of horses.

80   *dressed*, groomed.

85   *jade*, wretched nag.

86   *clapping*, patting.

88   *Since . . . fall*. A proverb from *Proverbs*, xvi. 18.

Runs posting on in Bolingbroke's proud joy,
While I stand fooling here, his jack of the clock.   60
This music mads me. Let it sound no more;
For though it have holp madmen to their wits,
In me it seems it will make wise men mad.
Yet blessings on his heart that gives it me,
For 'tis a sign of love; and love to Richard
Is a strange brooch in this all-hating world.

Enter a GROOM *of the stable*

GROOM: Hail royal prince.
RICHARD: Thanks noble peer.
  The cheapest of us is ten groats too dear.
  What art thou, and how comest thou hither,
  Where no man never comes but that sad dog   70
  That brings me food to make misfortune live?
GROOM: I was a poor groom of thy stable, King,
  When thou wert king; who travelling towards York
  With much ado at length have gotten leave
  To look upon my sometimes royal master's face.
  O how it earned my heart when I beheld
  In London streets, that coronation day,
  When Bolingbroke rode on roan Barbary,
  That horse that thou so often hast bestrid,
  That horse that I so carefully have dressed.   80
RICHARD: Rode he on Barbary? Tell me gentle friend,
  How went he under him?
GROOM: So proudly as if he disdained the ground.
RICHARD: So proud that Bolingbroke was on his back?
  That jade hath eat bread from my royal hand,
  This hand hath made him proud with clapping him.
  Would he not stumble, would he not fall down—
  Since pride must have a fall—and break the neck
  Of that proud man that did usurp his back?

90   *rail on*, speak abusively.

94   *galled*, chafed, made sore. *jauncing*, moving up and down with the horse's movement.

        Roan Barbary performs the function to which he was born and perhaps suggests the pride of royal state continuing with Bolingbroke now firmly in the saddle though a usurper. Richard, born to be king is now a mere beast bearing the burden of his sorrow.

95   s.d. *meat*, food.

99   *Taste . . . do.* As a protection against poison.

100–1 *My . . . contrary.* Prose. Some divide the lines after 'who'. Perhaps an alteration changed the original verse to prose.

105   *How . . . assault?* Even if 'means' is taken as 'meanest' the line is obscure. Perhaps 'death' should be emended to 'thou' on the assumption that the compositor's eye was influenced by 'death's' in the next line. *rude*, violent.

106   *thy . . . instrument.* According to Holinshed Richard seized a bill from one of the eight assailants and killed four of them.

107   *room*, place.

108–   *That . . . land.* Richard affirms his kingship and in the next speech
10   Exton acknowledges it.

109   *staggers*, causes to stagger.

Forgiveness, horse—why do I rail on thee,   90
Since thou, created to be awed by man,
Wast born to bear? I was not made a horse,
And yet I bear a burden like an ass,
Spurred, galled, and tired by jauncing Bolingbroke.

Enter KEEPER *to Richard with meat*

KEEPER: Fellow, give place, here is no longer stay.
RICHARD: If thou love me, 'tis time thou wert away.
GROOM: What my tongue dares not, that my heart shall say.

[*Exit*

KEEPER: My lord, will't please you to fall to?
RICHARD: Taste of it first as thou art wont to do.
KEEPER: My lord I dare not. Sir Piers of Exton,   100
Who lately came from the King, commands the contrary.
RICHARD: The devil take Henry of Lancaster, and thee!
Patience is stale, and I am weary of it.   [*Strikes the keeper*
KEEPER: Help, help, help!

Enter the murderers, EXTON *and servants*

RICHARD: How now, what means death in this rude assault?
Villain, thy own hand yields thy death's instrument.

[*He snatches a weapon from a servant and kills him*
Go thou and fill another room in hell.

[*He kills another servant. Then Exton strikes him down*
RICHARD: That hand shall burn in never-quenching fire
That staggers thus my person. Exton, thy fierce hand
Hath with the King's blood stained the King's own land. 110
Mount, mount, my soul, thy seat is up on high,
Whilst my gross flesh sinks downwards here to die.   [*Dies*

113– *As . . . hell.* Exton's remorse, according to Holinshed, caused him
16 to weep bitterly.

Does Richard—know himself, find love and loyalty, recover
royal presence, acknowledge failing, redeem himself, die in love
and charity?

Windsor Castle

A full ceremonial entry.

3 *Ciceter*, Cirencester.

8 *Spencer* F. Q has 'Oxford' who was not involved.

10 *At large discoursed*, narrated in full.

15 *consorted*, associated.

EXTON: As full of valour as of royal blood.
  Both have I spilled. O would the deed were good!
  For now the devil, that told me I did well,
  Says that this deed is chronicled in hell.
  This dead King to the living King I'll bear.
  Take hence the rest, and give them burial here.   [*Exeunt*

SCENE SIX

Flourish. Enter KING HENRY, *the* DUKE OF YORK,
other lords, and attendants

KING HENRY: Kind uncle York, the latest news we hear
  Is that the rebels have consumed with fire
  Our town of Ciceter in Gloucestershire,
  But whether they be ta'en or slain we hear not.

Enter NORTHUMBERLAND

  Welcome my lord. What is the news?
NORTHUMBERLAND: First, to thy sacred state wish I all
    happiness.
  The next news is, I have to London sent
  The heads of Salisbury, Spencer, Blunt, and Kent.
  The manner of their taking may appear
  At large discoursed in this paper here.   10
KING HENRY: We thank thee gentle Percy for thy pains;
  And to thy worth will add right worthy gains.

Enter FITZWATER

FITZWATER: My lord, I have from Oxford sent to London
  The heads of Brocas and Sir Bennet Seely,
  Two of the dangerous consorted traitors

16   *dire*, disastrous.

18   *wot*, know.

20   *clog*, burden. *sour melancholy*, bitter melancholic bile (i.e. causing disease).

23   *doom*, judgment.

25   *secret place*, obscure retreat. *reverend room*. Possibly place for religious meditation or observances.

26   *More . . . hast*, i.e. the small prison cell. *joy thy life*, rejoice that you are granted life.

30   s.d. A formal procession with the coffin effecting a striking *coup de théâtre*. What movements and gestures from the assembly are apt?

35   *slander*, shame. *fatal*, murderous.

38   *They . . . need*. Proverbially 'a king loves treason but hates the traitor'. Bolingbroke's rejection of Exton has many precedents.

That sought at Oxford thy dire overthrow.
KING HENRY: Thy pains Fitzwater shall not be forgot.
   Right noble is thy merit well I wot.

Enter PERCY *with the* BISHOP OF CARLISLE, *guarded*

PERCY: The grand conspirator Abbot of Westminster
   With clog of conscience and sour melancholy   20
   Hath yielded up his body to the grave.
   But here is Carlisle living to abide
   Thy kingly doom and sentence of his pride.
KING HENRY: Carlisle, this is your doom:
   Choose out some secret place, some reverend room
   More than thou hast, and with it joy thy life.
   So as thou livest in peace, die free from strife;
   For though mine enemy thou hast ever been,
   High sparks of honour in thee have I seen.

Enter EXTON *with the coffin*

EXTON: Great King, within this coffin I present   30
   Thy buried fear. Herein all breathless lies
   The mightiest of thy greatest enemies,
   Richard of Bordeaux, by me hither brought.
KING HENRY: Exton, I thank thee not, for thou hast wrought
   A deed of slander with thy fatal hand
   Upon my head and all this famous land.
EXTON: From your own mouth my lord, did I this deed.
KING HENRY: They love not poison that do poison need,
   Nor do I thee. Though I did wish him dead,
   I hate the murderer, love him murdered.   40
   The guilt of conscience take thou for thy labour,
   But neither my good word nor princely favour.
   With Cain go wander thorough shades of night,
   And never show thy head by day nor light.
   Lords, I protest my soul is full of woe

46 *That . . . grow.* See *Heb.*, xii. 24: 'And to Jesus the mediator of the new covenant, and to the blood of sprinkling, that speaketh better than did the blood of Abel'.

48 *incontinent*, immediately.

49 *I'll . . . Land.* Shakespeare takes up the theme of expiation by a crusade in *1* and *2 Henry IV*.

51 *grace*, honour, respect.

What effect is intended by the large amount of rhyme in this last scene?

What is an appropriate order for a ceremonial exit?

That blood should sprinkle me to make me grow.
Come mourn with me for what I do lament,
And put on sullen black incontinent.
I'll make a voyage to the Holy Land
To wash this blood off from my guilty hand.   50
March sadly after, grace my mournings here
In weeping after this untimely bier.   [*Exeunt*

APPENDICES

I

SOURCES AND INFLUENCES

EIGHT works have been suggested as sources for the play or as influencing it in some way, and to these Dover Wilson added an earlier play on Richard II no longer extant. The evidence for the use of this hypothetical play, and two French manuscripts by observers of Richard's fall, must be regarded as not proven. The tragic verse stories of the *Mirror for Magistrates* (1587) were certainly known to Shakespeare but there seem to be no specific parallels in the play. Hall's *Union of the Two Noble and Illustre Families of Lancaster and York* (1548) almost certainly provided Shakespeare with the overall pattern for his two cycles of history plays, but no close similarities of phrase occur. It is possible that Shakespeare drew hints from *The Chronicle of Froissart*, translated by Lord Berners (1525), for the character of Gaunt as a patriot, a wise counsellor, and a prophet, quite unlike the powerful, self-seeking, aggressive noble of the chronicles. Yet if Richard was to be portrayed as rejecting wise advice, it would be necessary to have a counsellor whose advice he could reject. The claims of a manuscript play *Woodstock*, or *I Richard II* have been strongly urged, particularly by Dover Wilson and A. P. Rossiter, and there are clear verbal and other resemblances between the two plays. Recently the arguments of G. Lambrechts, and the present writer's palaeographical knowledge of the play, and of the collection of manuscript plays to which it belongs, have persuaded him that it should be dated after *Richard II*, probably 1603–5.

It is most probable that Shakespeare was influenced by Daniel's verse history the *First Four Books of the Civil Wars* (1595). Only in Daniel's account is there a last meeting between Richard and the Queen (V. i) portrayed as a grown woman not as the girl of eleven she was historically.

Although Shakespeare differs in his handling of the matter, there are some verbal similarities, particularly lines 40–50. Richard's soliloquy in prison in Daniel has: 'Thou sit'st at home safe by thy quiet fire, And hear'st of others harms, but feelest none; and there thou tell'st of kings who aspire, Who fall, who rise, who triumphs, who do moan: Perhaps thou talk'st of me' (III. st. 65). Otherwise the soliloquy in Daniel is unlike that in the play. Shakespeare's main source is Holinshed's *Chronicles* (1587), which he follows fairly closely. For dramatic reasons he omits such matters as Richard's Irish campaign and the ambush whereby Northumberland trapped Richard and took him to Flint Castle. The events leading to the deposition are shortened and telescoped in time.

A number of things in the play have been added to the outline story. John of Gaunt's character is largely of Shakespeare's devising. The meeting between Gaunt and the Duchess of Gloucester (I. ii), Aumerle's parting from Bolingbroke (I. iv. 1–22), the Queen's grief (II. ii. 1–40), the Garden Scene (III. iv), the part played by the Duchess of York (V. ii, iii), Richard's soliloquy and conversation with the Groom (V. v. 1–94), the presentation of Richard's coffin to Bolingbroke, and the latter's intention to expiate the crime by a crusade are all Shakespeare's invention.

Shakespeare again enriched his narrative by such passages as Gaunt's praise of England, developed character by display of emotion as in Richard's wish to become an anchorite and to die, used allegory (Gardeners' scene), and symbol (mirror and crown).

Awareness of the changes and additions is helpful in trying to appreciate Shakespeare's intentions in the play.

II

QUEEN ELIZABETH AND WILLIAM LAMBARDE

ON 4 August 1601, Queen Elizabeth saw William Lambarde, the Keeper of the Records at the Tower of London, in her room at Greenwich. He presented an account of the records. As she examined them she 'fell upon the reign of King Richard II. saying, "I am Richard II. know ye not that?"

Feste, the clown, would wear the traditional fool's coat or petticoat of motley, a coarse cloth of mixed yellow and green. The coat was buttoned from the neck to the girdle from which hung a wooden dagger, its skirts voluminous with capacious pockets in which Feste might

A WOODCUT FROM R. FLUDD'S
Ars Memoria
possibly representing the Blackfriars Theatre

'impetticoat' any 'gratillity'. Ghosts who appear in a number of plays, usually wore a kind of leathern smock. Oberon and magicians such as Prospero wore, in the delightful phrase and spelling of the records, 'a robe for to goo invisibell'.

The actors formed companies under the patronage of noblemen for protection against civic law condemning them as 'rogues, vagabonds and sturdy beggars' to severe punishment. They were the servants of their patron and wore his livery. The company was a co-operative society, its members jointly owned the property and shared the profits; thus Shakespeare's plays were not his to use as he liked, they belonged to his company, the Lord Chamberlain's Men. This company, honoured by James I when it became the King's Men, was the most successful company of the period. It had a number of distinguished actors, it achieved more Court performances than any other company, and it performed in the best London theatre, the Globe, until it was burnt down during a performance of *Henry VIII* in 1613. Women were not allowed on the public stage, although they performed in masques and theatricals in private houses. Boys, therefore, were apprenticed to the leading actors and took the female parts.

An almost unbelievable number of plays was produced by the companies. It has been shown for example that in a fortnight eleven performances of ten different plays were presented by one company at one theatre. The companies were in effect repertory companies. Their productions consisted of new plays, and old plays either repeated without change, or revised sometimes extensively. It is to be wondered how far the actors achieved word-perfection in their parts. Their versatility and their team work no doubt helped to overcome the burden of such rapid changes of parts. Indeed although the main parts in a play were performed by a small select group of actors, there is little evidence of type-casting apart from the clowns, or that plays were written with particular actors in mind.

The audience in the public theatres was drawn from all classes. There were courtiers and inns of court men who appreciated intricate word play, mythological allusions, and the technique of sword play; there were the 'groundlings' who liked jigs, horse-play, and flamboyance of speech and spectacle; and there were the citizens who appreciated the romantic stories, the high eloquence of patriotic plays, and moral senti-

MODEL OF AN ELIZABETHAN THEATRE
by Richard Southern

ments. A successful play would have something for all. In private
theatres like the Blackfriars gallants would sit on a stool on the stage and
behave rather like the courtiers in *A Midsummer Night's Dream*, V. i, or
Love's Labour's Lost, V. ii. The 'groundlings' too were likely to be
troublesome and noisy. They could buy bottled beer, oranges, and nuts
for their comfort; but it is noted to their credit that when Falstaff
appeared on the stage, so popular was he that they stopped cracking
nuts! They applauded a well delivered speech; they hissed a boring play;
they even rioted and severely damaged one theatre. Shakespeare's plays
however were popular among all classes: at Court they

> did so take Eliza and our James,

and elsewhere in the public theatre they outshone the plays of other
dramatists. Any play of his was assured of a 'full house'. An ardent
theatre-goer of the day praising Shakespeare's plays above those of other
dramatists wrote:

> When let but Falstaff come,
> Hal, Poins, the rest, you scarce shall have a room,
> All is so pester'd; let but Beatrice
> And Benedick be seen, lo in a trice
> The cockpit, galleries, boxes, all are full
> To hear Malvolio, that cross-garter'd gull.

Shakespeare's Works

The year of composition of only a few of Shakespeare's plays can be determined with certainty. The following list is based on current scholarly opinion.

The plays marked with an asterisk were not included in the First Folio edition of Shakespeare's plays (1623) which was prepared by Heminge and Condell, Shakespeare's fellow actors. Shakespeare's part in them has been much debated.

1590–1   2 Henry VI, 3 Henry VI.

1591–2   1 Henry VI.

1592–3   Richard III, Comedy of Errors.

1593–4   Titus Andronicus, Taming of the Shrew, Sir Thomas More★ (Part authorship. Four manuscript pages presumed to be in Shakespeare's hand).

1594–5   Two Gentlemen of Verona, Love's Labour's Lost, Romeo and Juliet, Edward III★ (Part authorship).

1595–6   Richard II, A Midsummer Night's Dream.

1596–7   King John, Merchant of Venice, Love's Labour Won (Not extant. Before 1598).

1597–8   1 Henry IV, 2 Henry IV, The Merry Wives of Windsor.

1598–9   Much Ado About Nothing, Henry V.

1599–1600   Julius Caesar, As You Like It.

1600–1   Hamlet, Twelfth Night.

1601–2   Troilus and Cressida.

1602–3   All's Well that Ends Well.